WHAT will they LEARN? 2018-19

A Survey of Core Requirements at Our Nation's Colleges and Universities

American Council of Trustees and Alumni

FOREWORD

The image of a college student has steadily changed over the past few generations. The expectation of a college student used to be that of a "scholar" and a learned individual. Today, many colleges do not boast so much of their libraries, classrooms, or even their academic programs. Swimming pools, activity centers, and food courts tend to fill colleges' marketing publications. College outreach emphasizes amenities rather than the substance of teaching and learning. This phenomena has frustrated employers who struggle to find qualified employees. To ensure that students graduate prepared for meaningful careers, and, equally important, informed citizenship, higher education must reengage its purpose and dedicate itself to higher academic standards.

Ten years ago, the American Council of Trustees and Alumni (ACTA) gathered data on 100 colleges from the *U.S. News & World Report's* annual list of "Best Colleges and Universities." ACTA questioned whether these elite institutions were requiring their students to take rigorous, college-level courses in the core areas crucial for success. The results of this survey were dismal—showing that students could bypass essential courses that cultivate critical thinking, logic, writing skills, and mathematics, and revealing that American colleges are often failing to provide a truly collegiate education. If students are not taking college-level courses in core subjects, then what courses are they taking, and more importantly, *what are they learning*?

ACTA prepared this report, now in its 10th edition, to answer this question, of great concern to students, parents, and employers. Other ranking systems pit schools against each other in an effort to rank schools from "best" to "worst." These rankings focus on external inputs, such as alumni giving and admission selection, rather than on what actually happens in the classroom. ACTA, however, believes each school should be evaluated based on its academic substance—what fundamental skills and knowledge does the institution require of its students? Since our first survey, we have expanded our analysis to include over 1,100 colleges and universities in order to evaluate whether each individual school requires the essential areas of a liberal arts core curriculum.

The media and higher education institutions across the country have taken note. What Will They Learn?®'s research can be found in *TIME* magazine, *Times Higher Education*, and RealClearEducation. In 2015, What Will They Learn?®and ACTA received the Salvatori Prize for American Citizenship from the Heritage Foundation for our tireless work to improve higher education's curricular standards. Many universities have reached out to ACTA to design and reconstruct their core curricula after viewing our findings. In Virginia, Christopher Newport University (CNU) examined What Will They Learn?® to help shape CNU's current core curriculum and became the first public university to earn a perfect ACTA "A" rating. The University of Saint Katherine in California, which opened in 2011, based its core on ACTA standards to become an "A" school. The University of Science and Arts of Oklahoma used their "A" rating as a marketing tool to attract prospective students and their parents. An ACTA "A"—and even an ACTA "B"—matters, and continues to be a source of pride for many institutions.

And ACTA is expanding its reach and resources. We are forging a new path to put *What Will They Learn?* into the hands of college-bound students through the creation of a one-of-a-kind database of 40,000 private and public high school guidance counselors. This outreach initiative will provide high school guidance counselors, teachers, parents, and students with valuable tools for evaluating schools in the college selection process. Additional resources are available online at WhatWillTheyLearn.com. There, we offer information on a topic of increasing urgency: whether colleges and universities foster free speech and the free exchange of ideas, or instead capitulate to campus sensitivities and enact speech codes. We strive to hold schools accountable for maintaining academic freedom. ACTA believes that the college campus must be a forum in which to question, analyze, and critique opposing viewpoints.

So please, read on. And see how you—trustees, school leaders, policymakers, alumni, parents, guidance counselors, and students—can join ACTA in its efforts to ensure that a college diploma signifies a robust education that prepares all graduates for the very real challenges of career, community, and citizenship.

Dr. Michael Poliakoff
President

TABLE OF CONTENTS

Thomas Jefferson famously declared that ignorance and freedom do not exist together. His friend and ally James Madison envisioned liberty and learning leaning together for their mutual support. . . . Many of our Founders, including Patrick Henry, Benjamin Franklin, George Washington, Benjamin Rush, and John Dickinson, were themselves trustees or benefactors of institutions of higher learning: They saw such learning as essential for the new nation. And it remains essential today.

Dr. Michael Poliakoff
President, American Council of Trustees and Alumni

INTRODUCTION

The *Autobiography of Benjamin Franklin*, *Robinson Crusoe*, and *The Arabian Nights* were just some of the texts that influenced President Abraham Lincoln. President Barack Obama credits Joseph Conrad's 1899 novel *Heart of Darkness* as a vital text that helped him understand prejudice. Virgil's *Aeneid* motivated Facebook CEO and founder Mark Zuckerberg to create the largest social media platform in the world. Jane Austin's 1815 novel *Emma* had a personal impact on J.K. Rowling, the author of the Harry Potter series. Marc Benioff, the founder and co-CEO of salesforce.com, shared, "Since I first read *The Art of War* more than a dozen years ago, I have applied its concepts to many areas of my life . . . . Ultimately, it is how salesforce.com took on the entire software industry."[1]

Lincoln did not attend college, and Zuckerberg left Harvard University before finishing his degree. But for some students, college is the only place where they will be exposed to a number of such influential texts. Yet colleges and universities continue to offer unstructured and chaotic curricula, causing students to sort through a plethora of course options in the name of "choice" and "self-discovery." General education requirements are saturated with academic jargon that focuses more on vague learning outcomes than on the specific courses and topics that students need. As a result, students are left even more confused as to what they are supposed to learn. We find that hundreds of colleges, large and small, prestigious and not, require far less of their students than they should. During this rapidly changing period of history, American higher education overall does not adequately hold itself responsible for the intellectual and professional development of American citizens and America's workforce.

Now in its 10th anniversary, ACTA's *What Will They Learn?* report rates over 1,100 colleges and universities on whether or not they require a rigorous general education curriculum. What

Will They Learn?® establishes a clear, but also substantial, set of expectations: Composition, Literature, (intermediate-level) Foreign Language, U.S. Government or History, Economics, Mathematics, and Natural Science. A comprehensive general education ought to include courses outside a student's major that are tailored to equip him or her with the skills and knowledge needed to engage as a contributing member of the community and demonstrate value to future employers. *Forbes* magazine, for example, writes, "Having excellent writing skills can make you an indispensable member of your team or company. And it's one of the best ways to remain consistently employable—no matter your profession. Especially when you consider that workers can spend a third of their time reading and writing emails alone (according to a Carleton University study)."[2] Yet 18.7% of the schools we surveyed do not require a basic course in English composition.

The millennial generation is on track to becoming the largest educated generation in our nation's history. The United States Department of Education found that 1.9 million bachelor's degrees were awarded in the 2017–18 school year.[3] Of those 1.9 million, the greatest number of degrees were conferred in business, followed by health and medical-related professions.[4] In an increasingly competitive and educated global environment, a foundation in the liberal arts is the best way to ensure that students graduate with a comprehensive set of skills they can offer to their future employers and which will give them the intellectual agility they need for an ever-changing job market.

The study of a foreign language to the intermediate level, for example, can provide students with an exclusive skill. According to the U.S. Department of State, "The School of Language Studies (SLS), associated with the department's Foreign Service Institute, employs motivated individuals who are interested in making a difference in our relationships with other countries through the development of U.S. diplomats' foreign language skills. We look for applicants with expertise in second language acquisition, applied linguistics, and foreign language and adult education to train Department of State personnel for their real-world, high-stake jobs."[5]

Additionally, those with foreign language expertise fare better in the job market and often earn higher wages. A study by Rosetta Stone found that "people who speak at least one foreign language have an average annual income that's $10,000 higher than [the] household income of those who only speak English. And approximately 17 percent of those who speak at least one foreign language earn more than $100,000 a year."[6]

There is much that remains to be done. Since What Will They Learn?® began in 2009, institutions of higher education have only sporadically made improvements to their general education requirements. The University of California–Los Angeles and the University of Virginia, which earned a "C" and a "D" respectively in the 2009 *What Will They Learn?* report, now both receive an "F". And the number of "F" schools has reached a record high of 134, compared to 127 in the ninth edition and 118 in the eighth edition.

Thus, the results of the *What Will They Learn?* report reveal that many colleges and universities are overlooking the most essential part of a rigorous undergraduate education: a comprehensive core curriculum. Students require sound academic guidance from the colleges and universities they are trusting with their investments, but it is precisely there that too many institutions let them down. Students cannot expect to have impact on the world and their communities with a jumble of unrelated knowledge and skills. But for those who graduate with a firm foundation in the liberal arts, the opportunities for success are vast.

THE IMPORTANCE OF A CORE CURRICULUM

Over the course of the 2018–19 review, ACTA's research team read each mission statement of the general education curriculum of over 1,100 institutions. The vast majority of these institutions advertised on their websites and in their undergraduate catalogs that their general education programs are critical to their missions.

A rigorous general education program exposes students to a rich selection of college-level courses that they may not have the opportunity to experience after they select a major field of study. Taking a foundational set of core courses during the first and second years of college instruction can inspire students to pursue coursework in academic fields that they may not have considered before.

A recent PayScale study reported that "only 50% of managers think recent college graduates are prepared for the workforce."[7] Prominent higher education leaders such as Scott Millar, rector of Christopher Newport University, believe in the value of the core. Mr. Millar has shared that CNU's core curriculum gives their students "the ability to do anything once they graduate. . . . Over the next forty, forty-five, or fifty years of their work experience, they're likely to have a multitude of jobs in a variety of different disciplines. At the pace that we see rapid technology changes [and] changes in our society, it's important that students are being prepared not only for their first year or two out of school, but ten years from now [and] thirty years from now, because their career will expand in that period of time."[8]

Colleges and universities often trumpet their dedication to the liberal arts mission, while many fail to provide a true liberal arts education for their students. Take for example Kalamazoo College's mission statement "to prepare its graduates to better understand, live successfully within, and provide enlightened leadership to a richly diverse and increasingly complex world."[9]

Such an undertaking requires a liberal arts education, but Kalamazoo College earns an "F" from *What Will They Learn?*. The college only requires students to complete a handful of seminars and physical education courses. The wide gaps in Kalamazoo's required courses can prove costly as their students look toward future careers. Many other schools have similarly limited core curricula.

Other colleges and universities bundle essential subjects into broad distributional categories that provide too few college-level courses and instead allow students to fill their semesters with classes that provide little academic rigor or discovery. The University of California–Berkeley's core curriculum, in theory, has the skeleton structure of a decent core, but with over 300 course options fulfilling each requirement, students can bypass the majority of the seven core subjects deemed by ACTA and the scholars who advise us to be essential to a comprehensive liberal arts education. As a result, Berkeley receives an "F" rating.

We see this too often in course catalogs each year. Many colleges create cores that outline vague "ways of knowing" or "pathways" of courses that students can follow. These course catalogs use multiple pages to explain the outcomes of these distributions instead of providing clear course descriptions. As a result, students still do not have the knowledge or understanding of what courses they need to take. In an age when a high school education often fails to prepare students for college-level coursework, it is important to ensure that writing, literacy, mathematics, critical thinking, and analytical skills are clear requirements during the four years of college.

There are, of course, schools that differentiate themselves from their peers. There are both small liberal arts schools and large state flagships that do require more from their students. And for parents, financing a rigorous education does not have to break the bank. The University of Georgia, an ACTA "A" school, costs $11,818 annually in-state and $30,392 annually for out-of-state students, a sharp contrast to Middlebury College, an "F" school that costs students $52,496 each year. The University of Chicago requires an excellent humanities and civilization component embedded into their core curriculum that connects students to historical texts and exposes them to art, literature, and philosophy. The Great Books curriculum at St. John's College delves into the roots of classical education, requiring students to read, analyze, and discuss over 100 books during their four years.

With college costs rising and competition intensifying, the college search process can be daunting. But the failure of some schools to provide an enriching core should not discourage students from finding what they need. There are excellent universities in every region of the country that can provide a well-rounded education that is worth the price tag. Dr. Donald W. Sweeting, President of Colorado Christian University, states, "ACTA's rankings help students make choices in higher education that prepare them for this fast-changing marketplace and to be better citizens, as well."[10] And if a student does not attend a school with a strong core, he or she can still select rigorous courses at the institution in the seven core subjects outlined in this guide that are preparation for successful careers and enriching lives.

High school guidance counselors have a crucial role in this process, also. Directing students and their families toward resources other than overall rankings and glitzy student-life pamphlets can help students expand their college options to find a campus with a serious academic culture, as well as a place that is suited to their budgets and personal needs. If enough counselors, parents, and students begin voicing their concerns about educational outcomes, American colleges and universities will be motivated to rise to the occasion and improve their core curricula.

METHODOLOGY AND CRITERIA

There is no concrete or universal set of subjects that define the "liberal arts," but their aim has always been to impart the skills and knowledge needed for success in career and citizenship and to inspire understanding of the human condition. What Will They Learn?® asks whether or not schools require the study of seven subjects essential for a 21st-century liberal arts education. One could easily argue to include any number of additional topics: art, music, psychology, sociology, or philosophy, among many more. These subjects are certainly deserving of a student's attention, but a core curriculum that fails to require all, or at least most, of the seven key subjects outlined in this report clearly will not prepare students for professional life and educated civic engagement. Panels of distinguished professors and scholars have guided our criteria for what constitutes proper, college-level courses in these areas.

During the spring and summer of 2018, ACTA's curricular research team examined the undergraduate catalogs and other publicly available materials of over 1,100 colleges and universities to assess academic requirements. The team used the latest catalogs available online through the end of July. In cases where different units within the school had different requirements for various programs, we based our conclusions upon the requirements for baccalaureate degrees. If a subject was merely one of several options (as is often the case with so-called distribution requirements), or if a subject was optional for students in either the B.A. or B.S. program, the college or university did not receive credit. What Will They Learn?® does not grant credit for a subject if the institution uses SAT or ACT scores to exempt students from coursework, as an examination of high school-level skills is no replacement for collegiate requirements.

Our intent is to determine what institutions require of their students, not what they merely offer or suggest. Each year, ACTA sends a letter to the registrar and chief academic officer of every school we survey, asking for any updates to their curriculum and for their review of our past ratings for accuracy.

1. Composition

The ability to write clearly and effectively is among the most fundamental of academic skills, and is critical for advanced work in all fields. It is also a subject that takes a lifetime to master, so students who arrive at college with adequate writing skills still benefit from improving them.

What Will They Learn?® gives schools credit for Composition if they require an introductory college writing class focusing on grammar, clarity, argument, and appropriate expository style. Remedial courses may not be used to satisfy a composition requirement. University-administered exams or portfolios are acceptable only when they are used to determine exceptional pre-college preparation for students. Writing-intensive courses, "writing across the curriculum" seminars, and writing for a

discipline are acceptable when there are clear provisions for multiple writing assignments, instructor feedback, revision and resubmission of student writing, and attention to the mechanics of formal writing.

2. Literature

The ability to read the great works of literature enables students to analyze complex and subtle language and explore the diversity of human thought and experience. Forming habits of attentive reading and reflection imparts cognitive gains that students will use for the rest of their lives. It is fundamental training for the critical thinking skills that are so important for all careers. In many cases, college marks the last time students will read books they do not choose themselves, making it even more urgent to offer this core educational experience.

What Will They Learn?® awards schools credit for Literature when they require a comprehensive survey of written literary texts or offer a selection of courses of which a clear majority are surveys and the remainder focus on written literary texts, even if single-author or theme-based in structure. Freshman seminars count, as do humanities sequences or other specialized courses that include a substantial literature survey component.

3. Foreign Language

There is no better tool for understanding the perspectives of different cultures than the study of foreign languages. To learn a culture's history or art or traditions is secondhand knowledge; to learn its language is the first step to true understanding. In an increasingly interconnected world, competency in a foreign language molds students into informed participants in the international community—and makes them highly prized employees.

What Will They Learn?® awards credit for Foreign Language if schools require competency at the intermediate level, defined as at least three semesters of college-level study in any foreign language. This requirement must apply to all liberal arts degrees, without distinction between B.A. and B.S. degrees, or individual majors within these degrees. Credit also is awarded to schools that require two semesters each of college-level study in two different ancient languages.

4. U.S. Government or History

Higher educational institutions have a civic duty in a free society. Colleges and universities must ensure that students have a working knowledge of the history, governing documents, and governing institutions of their country. An understanding of American history and government is indispensable for the development of responsible citizens and for the preservation of free institutions.

What Will They Learn?® gives schools credit for U.S. Government or History if they require a survey course in either U.S. government or history with enough chronological and/or topical breadth to expose students to the sweep of American history and institutions. Narrow, niche courses that focus only on a limited chronological period or topic do not count for the requirement. Rigorous state- or university-administered exams are accepted as a substitute for coursework.

5. Economics

In an interconnected world of finite resources, understanding the principles that govern the allocation of goods and services—economics—is essential. Although economics has not traditionally been a part of the liberal arts core, informed citizenship in the 21st century requires instruction in economic principles and the fundamentals of the marketplace.

What Will They Learn?® awards credit for Economics if schools require a course covering basic economic principles, generally an introductory micro- or macroeconomics course taught by faculty from the economics or business department.

6. Mathematics

Just as studying the world of human culture requires language, studying the natural world and the social sciences requires mathematics. Scholars of ancient and medieval times understood that math provides a fundamentally different way of apprehending the world than that of language; it still does. Moreover, numeracy at the college level has practical benefits for everything from succeeding in the workplace to managing home finances to evaluating statistics found in the newspaper. Fairfield University eloquently states that mathematics is "both an object of abstract beauty and a model of deductive reasoning" and that calculus is especially appropriate for college-level study since it occupies "a unique place in Western intellectual history."[11]

What Will They Learn?® gives schools credit for Mathematics if they require a college-level course in mathematics. Specific topics may vary but must involve study beyond the level of intermediate algebra and cover topics beyond those typical of a college-preparatory high school curriculum. Remedial courses may not be used as substitutes. Courses in formal or symbolic logic, computer science with significant programming, and linguistics involving formal analysis count.

7. Natural Science

Familiarity with quantitative reasoning prepares students to master the basic principles of scientific experimentation and observation that are essential for understanding the world in which we live. Science courses such as chemistry, biology, and physics build the analytical and critical thinking skills that today's employers demand while preparing graduates to navigate the complex and interconnected world that they will join upon finishing their education.

What Will They Learn?® gives schools credit for Natural Science if they require a course in astronomy, biology, chemistry, geology, physical geography, physics, or environmental science, preferably with a laboratory component. Courses with weak scientific content, and courses taught by faculty outside of the science departments do not count. Psychology courses count if they are focused on the biological, chemical, or neuroscientific aspects of the field.

Half-Credit

If a requirement exists from which students choose between otherwise qualifying courses within two What Will They Learn?® subject areas (e.g., math or science, history or economics, etc.), half-credit is given for each subject.

Grading System

What Will They Learn?® assigns a grade to each institution based on how many of the following seven core subjects it requires students to complete.

The grading system is as follows:

A	6–7 subjects required
B	4–5 subjects required
C	3 subjects required
D	2 subjects required
F	0–1 subject required

Additional Information About Institutions in What Will They Learn?®

In addition to evaluations of general education requirements, What Will They Learn?® provides four-year graduation rates and tuition costs drawn from data available on the U.S. Department of Education's Integrated Postsecondary Education Data System (IPEDS). The figures from IPEDS include preliminary "early release" data and may be subject to revision.

The Website: WhatWillTheyLearn.com

Accompanying this printed report is a website by the same name, WhatWillTheyLearn.com. There one can find the information in this publication as well as a letter from former Harvard College Dean Harry Lewis; answers to frequently asked questions; detailed notes about the evaluation of subjects at individual schools; information wherever available on speech codes at each institution; and statements from each institution regarding general education. The website also includes press coverage of the project and copies of the Roper survey on Americans' support of a core curriculum, the Roper survey of American historical literacy among recent college graduates, the GfK survey of knowledge of the history of Theodore Roosevelt and Franklin Delano Roosevelt, and a survey of knowledge of the U.S. Constitution. Newly added to our website are the Heterodox Academy Guide to Colleges rankings and the Foundation for Individual Rights in Education (FIRE) speech code ratings for various colleges and universities.

KEY FINDINGS

What Will They Learn?® evaluates every four-year public university with a stated liberal arts mission as well as hundreds of private colleges and universities selected on the basis of size, mission, and regional representation. All schools in the What Will They Learn?® study are regionally accredited, nonprofit institutions. Combined, the over 1,100 institutions in the What Will They Learn?® study enroll nearly 8 million students, more than two-thirds of all students enrolled in four-year liberal arts schools nationwide.

Overall, the results are troubling. The grade tally tells the story:

A 23 (2%)

B 343 (31%)

C 347 (31%)

D 273 (24%)

F 134 (12%)

Less than half of the schools studied require:

Literature – 34%
Foreign Language – 12%
U.S. Government or History – 17%
Economics – 3%

WHAT WILL THEY LEARN® GRADE BREAKDOWN

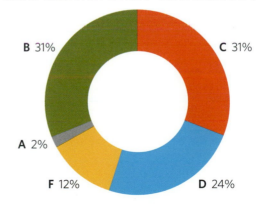

B 31% C 31%

A 2%

F 12% D 24%

WHAT WILL THEY LEARN?®
GRADE BREAKDOWN BY REGION

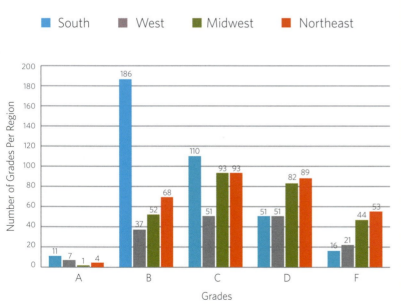

WHAT WILL THEY LEARN?®
SUBJECT AREA BREAKDOWN: PRIVATE VS. PUBLIC

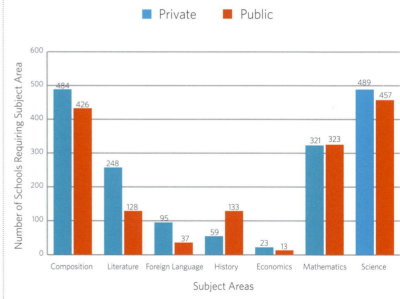

Although the style and content of general education programs vary greatly from institution to institution, the evaluation process has yielded several general observations:

■ **What a college promises often isn't what it practices.**
On the whole, higher education has abandoned a coherent content-rich general education curriculum. In their course catalogs and mission statements, colleges frequently exalt the virtues of a "well-rounded" liberal arts education. The reality, however, is that 67.5% of the schools surveyed require three or fewer of the seven core subjects. Their diffuse curricula poorly represent critical subjects like American history, economics, and foreign languages.

Often, schools do not hold themselves accountable to the mission they promote. Rice University in Texas states that their liberal arts education program allows students to "gain an understanding of the literature, arts, and philosophy essential to any civilization, a broad historical introduction to thought about human society, and a basic familiarity with the scientific principles underlying physics, chemistry, and mathematics."[12] And yet, Rice students can graduate without taking any What Will They Learn?®

college-level courses. Rice's broad distribution categories fail to provide students with a substantive "well-rounded" education.

■ **Money is no guarantee of a good core.**
This report makes clear that cost is a poor indicator of the strength of a school's core curriculum. Students attending *U.S. News*'s top national universities and liberal arts colleges are typically paying well over $40,000 each year in tuition and fees, but some of these schools require none of the seven core subjects. In sharp contrast, public universities—where the median in-state tuition and fees are a fraction of that amount—require an average of over three. An encouraging finding is that public colleges and universities generally do a better job maintaining requirements in science and English composition than do private institutions, and historically black colleges and universities are noteworthy for their strong requirements. And, our military service academies also have outstanding, rigorous requirements. Michael F. Adams, president emeritus of the University of Georgia, asserts the responsibility of public universities to provide a rigorous core: "Even in this modern age, students need exposure to English, high level math,

lab sciences, a foreign language, and strong social sciences. Such subjects will allow students to truly become citizens of this modern world."[13] One of the most expensive institutions studied, Bowdoin College, charges $51,848 in tuition and fees but only requires one of our seven core subjects. The average tuition and fees at the 23 "A" schools that charge tuition is $22,470, significantly less than most of the private universities in the study. A distressing paradox is that among the schools receiving an "F" from What Will They Learn?®, the average tuition is approximately $35,080, which brings into question the value of their educational offerings.

College administrators should note that it doesn't necessarily take more money to produce a terrific education. In fact, colleges and universities can save a hefty part of their instructional budget simply by reducing the number of course options that now fulfill general education requirements and concentrating efforts on providing first-rate instruction in a carefully chosen set of core offerings. According to ACTA's publication *The Cost of Chaos in the Curriculum*, "Eliminating general education courses that are not central to any discipline and are therefore not requirements of any major would save an institution an estimated 10% of its

instructional costs per semester—or more, depending on the university."[14] Thus, reducing the curriculum bloat can also reduce budget constraints.

Effective, efficient core curricula improve educational quality while lowering costs of instruction. The basic general education core that every student needs can be delivered much more cost-effectively than the array of niche and boutique courses so often offered as "distribution requirements" in lieu of a well-defined core. Especially in these hard economic times, governing boards of public colleges and universities risk legislative intervention if they cannot maintain the curricular standards and efficiencies that the public deserves and increasingly demands.

■ **Reputation isn't everything.**
Many college ratings attach great significance to a school's reputation. This circular logic ensures that the schools at the top of the rankings are those that everyone already "knows" are the best. Looking objectively at the facts, however, yields surprises.

The list of schools that received "A" grades includes some schools like Pepperdine and Baylor, renowned for their commitment to the liberal arts and academic excellence, but there are also rising stars that deserve to be better known, such as Christopher Newport University, Colorado Christian University, Kennesaw State University, Bluefield College, and Regent University. CNU President Paul Trible states, "At Christopher Newport University, we offer such a curriculum, which ACTA has consistently rated as one of the best of any university in the country. We believe that a rich and rigorous general education curriculum does more than simply produce well-rounded, knowledgeable graduates. It also gives students the opportunities to discover strengths and abilities, which increases their marketability, regardless of their major. And it encourages these students to become engaged citizens and leaders, ready to live lives of significance by positively impacting the world around them."[15]

The "F" list includes such august names as Berkeley, Bowdoin, Hamilton, and Vassar. That some of the best-known colleges earn poor marks for general education doesn't mean they don't do other things well. But what is clear is that many highly regarded universities enroll some of our nation's top students and then give them nothing more than a "do-it-yourself" core curriculum.

The famous Ivy League, for instance, is home to two "Bs," four "Cs," one "D," and one "F." These grades overall reflect significant curricular weaknesses. Yale does not require its students to take college-level math; Harvard accepts elementary-level study of a foreign language; and Brown has an "open curriculum," meaning students may take whatever classes they wish, with no core curriculum requirements at all.

Certainly, a student can get an excellent education at these schools if he or she chooses classes wisely. What our study reveals, however, is that instead of holding outstanding students to a high standard, the "big names" often let students take obscure, esoteric, and sometimes lightweight classes in place of a rigorous, coherent liberal arts core.

■ **Distribution requirements are requirements in name only.** While distribution requirements seem like an appealing idea on paper, in practice they usually allow students to graduate with only a thin and patchy education. Students may have dozens or even hundreds of courses from which to choose, many of them highly specialized niche courses. Once distribution requirements become too loose, students almost inevitably graduate with an odd list of random, unconnected courses and, all too often, serious gaps in their basic skills and knowledge. For example:

- University of Michigan: "Global X: Zombies!" fulfills the "Humanities" requirement.
- Linfield College: Students can fulfill either the "U.S. Pluralisms" or the "Individuals, Systems, and Society" requirement with "The Economics of Star Trek."
- DePaul University: "History of Comics" and "Game Design for Non-Majors" fulfill the "Arts and Literature" requirement.

■ **Legislatures, regents, and trustees can make a difference.** In some states, legislatures have created strong requirements for the study of U.S. history and government. For example, Texas state law requires that all public universities teach courses on American history and government; accordingly, every public institution in Texas receives credit for U.S. Government or History in *What Will They Learn?*®. So also Georgia: In accordance with legislation, all students at public institutions must demonstrate an understanding of U.S. and state history and constitutions. It is clear, however, that great vigilance is needed in upholding such state laws. A similar statute in California stipulates that all schools in the California State University system "require comprehensive study of American history and American government" as a condition of graduation.

Regents and trustees have also taken the initiative to create comprehensive general education standards, as seen in states including Tennessee, South Dakota, Georgia, Florida, and Nevada, where those requirements apply to all schools within a system or even a state. In Georgia, for example, the Board of Regents of the University System of Georgia (USG) has established statewide core curriculum guidelines. The result: The 19 institutions governed by the USG require an average of 4.5 of the seven subjects surveyed in *What Will They Learn?*®, well above the national average of 3. Similar results can be found at the universities under the jurisdiction of the Tennessee Board of Regents, the Oklahoma State Regents, and the Nevada Board of Regents. An added benefit: System-wide general education requirements facilitate transfers between the two- and four-year schools, substantially increasing the chances that a college student will receive a comprehensive education and complete it within four years.

■ **College catalogs conceal much about educational quality.**
Most of the research for this study was done by examining the information colleges and universities make available online, in much the same way a prospective student would. What we found was that students, parents, and policymakers trying to find out what schools require will often have a hard time of it. Some schools are clear and unambiguous about their requirements, but others have them scattered throughout the catalog. Some schools may have differing "core" curricula depending on students' majors, the divisions in which they are enrolled, or even the campuses on which they attend class. Shockingly, some schools do not issue their updated course catalogs until well into the summer, long past the time when students should begin to think carefully about their academic schedules for the coming year. More problematic yet, many catalogs do a poor job of describing courses. Very often, course descriptions include phrases such as "topics may include," followed by a broad list. The "may" means

that nobody—not parents, not students—can really know what is going to be covered. It will vary from section to section, semester to semester, depending on what a given instructor wishes to teach. The class might require serious, college-level work . . . or it might not.

Finally, colleges must stop allowing exemption from crucial courses on the basis of college entrance examinations. The ACT and SAT exams measure college readiness: They were never intended to measure mastery of collegiate skills. Allowing exemption from a college-level writing course on the basis of these test scores, at times as low as a 510 SAT writing score or a 22 on the ACT English section (University of the Pacific), or a 600 SAT mathematics score (Aurora University), is a disservice to students.

■ **American higher education needs to become serious about equipping students to be effective participants in global conversations and a global economy.**
Nearly every college and university we studied had some sort of diversity requirement, with the expectation that students are expected to learn about people different from themselves. This is a

commendable and excellent idea in our increasingly interconnected world. Surely, though, the best way to understand another culture is to know its language; students who can speak and read a foreign language competently are able to enter into another culture more deeply and can continue to do so throughout their lives. Yet less than 12% of the schools we studied require students to learn a foreign language at the intermediate level. Some allow elementary study of the kind typically required in high school to suffice; others have no requirement at all. Some allow classes in both American and foreign cultures taught in English. At Olivet College, for example, students can substitute for foreign language study courses titled "Childhood and Culture" and "Music and Culture"[16]; and at South Dakota State, courses such as "Three Dimensional Design" and "Film as Art" fill the same requirement as foreign language study, allowing students to bypass foreign language entirely.[17]

■ **When the study of American government and history are badly neglected in general education requirements, America's institutions and principles suffer.**

Despite the boasts of college catalogs, few of their curricula actively prepare students to be informed and engaged citizens. This year's survey showed that fewer than 18% of our colleges and universities require even a single foundational course in U.S. Government or History. The grim results of this curricular frivolity are arguably apparent in the nationwide instances of campus unrest. When institutions of higher learning neglect to require the study of our nation's most basic and cherished principles protected in the Constitution, they let ignorance supplant reasoned discourse. The Knight Foundation found that 10% of college students say using violence to prevent someone from speaking is sometimes acceptable, and 37% believe that shouting down speakers is sometimes acceptable. What may be even more alarming is that 36% of college students do not feel that the protection of free speech under the First Amendment is secure.[18] As W.E.B. DuBois warned in 1906, "Either the United States will destroy ignorance, or ignorance will destroy the United States."[19]

■ **The American public continues to stress the importance of economics, but hardly any universities require its study.**

Colleges and universities constantly profess that they seek to construct a curriculum that will address the particular needs of students in the 21st century. The Panetta Institute for Public Policy reported in 2016 that economic affairs ranked as the issue of highest importance for college graduates when they considered presidential candidates.[20] Yet despite the increasing importance of economics, just over 3% of the institutions studied require students to take a basic economics class.

■ **Employers and the public stress the importance of STEM, but many colleges and universities are failing to live up to these standards.**
The National Survey of America's College Students found that 20% of college students completing four-year degrees could not reliably "calculate the total cost of ordering office supplies."[21] This should be no surprise since only 58% of colleges and universities require students to take a college-level mathematics class. In 2015, the Committee for Economic Development reported that "quantitative and analytical skills/critical thinking" were among the top seven most desired skills in potential hires.[22] Moreover, the National Federation of Independent Businesses reported that, in the spring of 2015, 47% of small businesses hiring for available positions said there were "few or no qualified applicants."[23] The

skills gap in STEM fields will only continue to widen if significant numbers of colleges and universities continue to require mathematics courses below the college level or no coursework at all.

■ **There are some curious selections in the cafeteria line.**
Many colleges and universities continue to stress the importance of students building foundational knowledge and skills, but allow those students to satisfy these requirements with an incoherent curriculum. This is commonly called a "cafeteria-style" curriculum. The following are a few of the more peculiar general education classes we found in our research:

- Oberlin College: "New Zealand Film" fulfills the "Cultural Diversity" requirement.

- Stockton University: "Vampires: History of the Undead" fulfills the "Historical Consciousness" requirement.

- "U.S. History: The History of Food" and "U.S. History: America Through Sport" fulfill the "U.S. Government or History" requirement at Lindenwood University.

SOLUTIONS

Studies like the federal government's National Assessment of Adult Literacy and *What's a Parent to Do? How to Help Your Child Select the Right College* tell us beyond a shadow of a doubt that many college students invest a lot of time and money in higher education, but gain very little that would qualify as a reasonable return. Admittedly, the solutions to the problem are nuanced and multifaceted. But obtaining a baccalaureate degree that signifies real learning is surely a place to start. Moving away from the diffuse array of courses that now passes as general education to a real core curriculum is clearly the start to such a solution. It is nothing short of essential if American graduates expect to compete effectively in the global marketplace. Here are the initial steps needed to make it happen:

Colleges and universities must make improving general education an urgent priority. There are ample opportunities to do so. A 2011 Roper survey (see WhatWillTheyLearn.com) made it clear that an overwhelming majority of adults believe a sound core curriculum is very important and that those just out of college understand the need for rigorous preparation as they face the harsh realities of the marketplace. However, "curricular change" does not necessarily mean "curricular improvement." Parents, alumni, and trustees can be important voices for reform, and they must be informed and vigilant. As the president of Colorado Christian University states, "There is chaos in the curriculum of many universities and ACTA has a credible plan to not only bring some coherence and sanity back to your school, but to create a better foundation under the feet of the coming generation of students."[24]

High school guidance counselors, in their consultations with prospective college students and their families, must place academic excellence, cost, and freedom of inquiry and expression at the forefront of the college search process. Counselors should make resources focusing on ratings like What Will They Learn?® and Heterodox Academy's Guide to Colleges readily available to their students. Only when the consumers of higher education have access to valuable information about the true priorities of a college education, those that have a lasting impact on their futures, will baccalaureate providers begin to reinvigorate American higher education institutions.

Students and parents should vote with their wallets for the institutions that provide a sound foundation. The ratings in this book are also available at WhatWillTheyLearn.com, a free resource that is continually updated and expanded. While there are many questions to ask before choosing a college, "What will they learn?" is surely among the most essential. If students and their parents place more emphasis on education rather than reputation, institutions will respond.

Alumni and donors should take an active interest in the strength of their alma maters' general education programs. They should not allow their degrees to be devalued by a decline in standards, and they can speak up against lowering standards.

While donors cannot and should not dictate curricula, they can direct their gifts toward programs and institutions that share their values and priorities.

Boards of trustees, in collaboration with faculty members, should insist on a course of study that will ensure students learn the essentials: This means general education curricula characterized by meaningful requirements, satisfied by a select number of courses. Without leadership from trustees and administrators, internal campus decision-making often makes for a fragmented and ineffective curriculum. While curricular change may make some faculty and departments unhappy, it is critical in providing students the education they need.

In 2014, 21 of the nation's most distinguished college presidents, trustees, and policymakers met under the leadership of former Yale University president and City University of New York board chair Benno Schmidt. In their published report, *Governance for a New Era: A Blueprint for Higher Education Trustees*, they called upon trustees to reexamine their institutions' general education programs and to push back against the costly proliferation of classes offered in lieu of a rigorous core curriculum. ACTA's *Restoring a Core* trustee guide shows how trustees can work in partnership with faculty and administrators to institute meaningful general education requirements.[25]

Government officials should take note of the state of the college curricula at the institutions they oversee and support. While elected officials must never interfere in the classroom, they can and should ask questions about what their universities are doing to ensure that students get a well-rounded education.

Policymakers should also focus on the budgetary advantages of a high-quality core curriculum. Small, highly specialized courses have their place as electives, but they are not suitable for a core that is simultaneously substantive, cost-effective, and academically effective. Educational quality will go up as the costs go down when a sound core forms the heart of a well-planned, coherent undergraduate academic experience.

NOTES

1. Kristen Bahler, "13 Successful People on the Books That Changed Their Lives," *TIME*, September 27, 2017, http://time.com/money/4956231/ceos-favorite-books/.

2. Greta Solomon, "Why Mastering Writing Skills Can Help Future-Proof Your Career," *Forbes*, August 9, 2018, https://www.forbes.com/sites/gretasolomon/2018/08/09/why-mastering-writing-skills-can-help-future-proof-your-career/#6ac267b15831.

3. Integrated Postsecondary Education Data System (IPEDS), Degrees Conferred Projection Model, Degrees conferred by postsecondary institutions, by level of degree and sex of student: Selected years, 1869–70 through 2026–27, https://nces.ed.gov/programs/digest/d16/tables/dt16_318.10.asp.

4. National Center for Education Statistics, *Digest of Education Statistics: 2016*, "Postsecondary Education," https://nces.ed.gov/programs/digest/d16/ch_3.asp.

5. U.S. Department of State, Foreign Service Institute, School of Language Studies, Employment, https://www.state.gov/m/fsi/sls/employment/index.htm.

6. Live A Language Foundation, "Career Preparation: Multilingualism Career Advantages," 2018, http://livealanguage.org/programs/career-preparation/.

7. PayScale, "2016 Workforce Skills Preparedness Report," 2016, https://www.payscale.com/data-packages/job-skills.

8. Scott Millar, interview with the American Council of Trustees and Alumni (ACTA), August 2018.

9. Kalamazoo College, "Introduction and Mission," 2017, http://www.kzoo.edu/about/.

10. Donald W. Sweeting, email correspondence with ACTA, August 31, 2018.

11. Fairfield University, "Core Requirements," Academics, 2017, https://www.fairfield.edu/undergraduate/academics/the-core/requirements/#section-mathematics-open.

12. Rice University, "Undergraduate Students," 2018, https://ga.rice.edu/undergraduate-students/.

13. Michael F. Adams, email correspondence with ACTA, September 5, 2018.

14. Elizabeth D. Capaldi Phillips & Michael B. Poliakoff, *The Cost of Chaos in the Curriculum,* (Washington, DC: American Council of Trustees and Alumni, 2015), https://www.goacta.org/images/download/The_Cost_of_Chaos_in_the_Curriculum.pdf.

15. Paul Trible, correspondence with ACTA, August 31, 2018.

16. Olivet College, 2016–17 Academic Catalog, 68, https://www.olivetcollege.edu/wp-content/uploads/2016/10/2016-2017-Academic-Catalog_0.pdf.

17. South Dakota State University, "General Education Requirements," 2018–2019 Undergraduate Catalog, SGR Goal #4, http://catalog.sdstate.edu/content.php?catoid=34&navoid=5244#sgr1.

18. Gallup/Knight Foundation Survey, *Free Expression on Campus: What College Students Think About First Amendment Issues*, 2018, 2–5, https://kf-site-production.s3.amazonaws.com/publications/pdfs/000/000/248/original/Knight_Foundation_Free_Expression_on_Campus_2017.pdf.

19. W.E.B. DuBois, speech to the Niagara Movement (1906), "Men of Niagara," BlackPast.org, http://www.blackpast.org/1906-w-e-b-dubois-men-niagara.

20. Hart Research Associates, *2016 Survey of America's College Students* (Washington, DC: The Panetta Institute for Public Policy, 2016).

21. W. Robert Connor and Cheryl Ching, "Can Learning Be Improved When Budgets Are in the Red?," *The Chronicle of Higher Education*, April 25, 2010, http://chronicle.com/article/Can-Learning-Be-Improved-When/65229/; see also Sheida White and Sally Dillow, *Key Concepts and Features of the 2003 National Assessment of Adult Literacy*, (Washington, DC: U.S. Department of Education, 2005), 1–7, http://nces.ed.gov/NAAL/PDF/2006471.pdf.

22. Monica Herk, "The Skills Gap and the Seven Skill Sets that Employers Want: Building the Ideal New Hire," *Committee for Economic Development*, June 11, 2015, https://www.ced.org/blog/entry/the-skills-gap-and-the-seven-skill-sets-that-employers-want-building-the-id.

23. William C. Dunkelberg and Holly Wade, *Small Business Economic Trends,* (Nashville: National Federation of Independent Businesses, May 2015).

24. Donald W. Sweeting, email correspondence with ACTA, August 31, 2018.

25. Benno C. Schmidt, *Governance for a New Era: A Blueprint for Higher Education Trustees*, (Washington, DC: American Council

of Trustees and Alumni, 2014), https://www.goacta.org/images/download/governance_for_a_new_era.pdf; and *Restoring a Core: How Trustees Can Ensure Meaningful General Education Requirements* (Washington, DC: American Council of Trustees and Alumni, 2008), https://www.goacta.org/images/download/restoring_a_core.pdf.

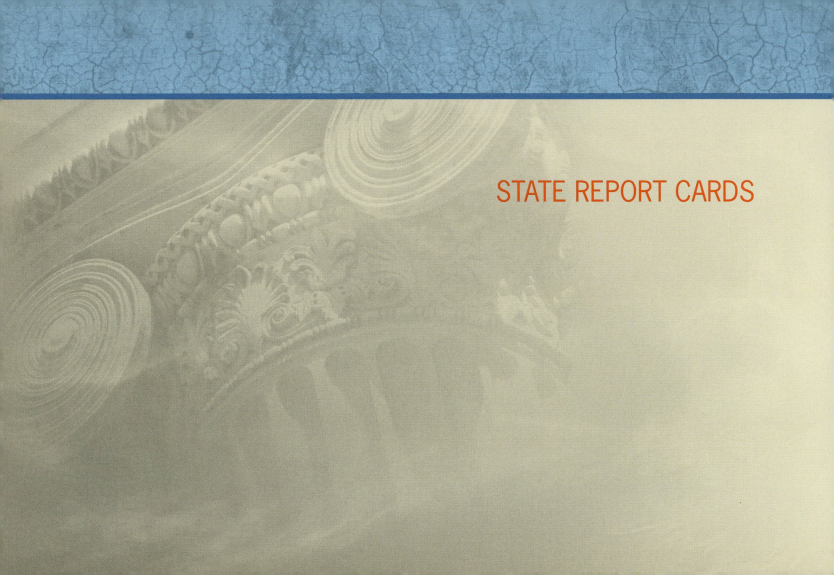

STATE REPORT CARDS

ALABAMA

GENERAL EDUCATION REQUIREMENTS

INSTITUTION	Comp	Lit	Lang	Gov/Hist	Econ	Math	Sci	GRADE	Tuition & Fees* (In-State/Out-of-State)	Graduation** Rate (4-Year)
Alabama A&M University	•	•			•	•	•	B	$9,857 / $18,236	4%
Alabama State University	•	•				•	•	B	$11,068 / $19,396	11%
Auburn University–Auburn		•				•	•	C	$10,968 / $29,640	49%
Auburn University–Montgomery	•	•				•	•	B	$8,020 / $17,140	9%
Birmingham-Southern College	•						•	D	$35,804	58%
Faulkner University	•	•				•	•	B	$20,970	12%
Huntingdon College	•	•				•	•	B	$26,400	27%
Jacksonville State University		•				•	•	C	$8,166 / $15,582	14%
Oakwood University	•						•	D	$16,720	24%
Samford University	•	•				•	•	B	$30,490	65%
Spring Hill College	•	•		•		•	•	B	$37,584	44%
Stillman College	•			•		•	•	B	$10,792	20%
Talladega College	•			•			•	C	$12,340	23%
Troy University		•				•	•	C	$8,692 / $16,276	19%
Tuskegee University	•	•				•	•	B	$22,170	28%

*   2017–18 tuition and fees. Source: U.S. Department of Education's Integrated Postsecondary Education Data System (IPEDS).
** Four-year graduation rates for first-time, full-time freshmen who enrolled in Fall 2011. Source: College Navigator.

GENERAL EDUCATION REQUIREMENTS

INSTITUTION	Comp	Lit	Lang	Gov/ Hist	Econ	Math	Sci	GRADE	Tuition & Fees (In-State/Out-of-State)	Graduation Rate (4-Year)
University of Alabama–Birmingham	●	●				●	●	B	$8,328 / $19,032	32%
University of Alabama–Huntsville	●	●				●	●	B	$10,280 / $21,480	23%
University of Alabama–Tuscaloosa	●	●				●	●	B	$10,780 / $28,100	44%
University of Montevallo	●					●	●	C	$12,400 / $25,030	26%
University of North Alabama	●	●				●	●	B	$8,480 / $15,128	20%
University of South Alabama	●	●				●	●	B	$7,812 / $15,324	19%
University of West Alabama	●	●				●	●	B	$9,204 / $16,818	18%

ALASKA

GENERAL EDUCATION REQUIREMENTS

INSTITUTION	Comp	Lit	Lang	Gov/ Hist	Econ	Math	Sci	GRADE	Tuition & Fees* (In-State/Out-of-State)	Graduation** Rate (4-Year)
Alaska Pacific University	●						●	D	$20,760	47%
University of Alaska–Anchorage							●	F	$6,690 / $19,494	8%
University of Alaska–Fairbanks						●	●	D	$6,262 / $19,183	20%
University of Alaska–Southeast						●	●	D	$6,828 / $19,533	10%

* 2017–18 tuition and fees. Source: U.S. Department of Education's Integrated Postsecondary Education Data System (IPEDS).
** Four-year graduation rates for first-time, full-time freshmen who enrolled in Fall 2011. Source: College Navigator.

ARIZONA

GENERAL EDUCATION REQUIREMENTS

INSTITUTION	Comp	Lit	Lang	Gov/Hist	Econ	Math	Sci	GRADE	Tuition & Fees* (In-State/Out-of-State)	Graduation** Rate (4-Year)
Arizona State University	●					●	●	C	$10,792 / $27,372	45%
Northern Arizona University	●					●	●	C	$11,059 / $24,841	40%
Prescott College	●							F	$30,501	2%
University of Arizona	●						●	D	$11,877 / $35,307	45%

* 2017–18 tuition and fees. Source: U.S. Department of Education's Integrated Postsecondary Education Data System (IPEDS).
** Four-year graduation rates for first-time, full-time freshmen who enrolled in Fall 2011. Source: College Navigator.

ARKANSAS

GENERAL EDUCATION REQUIREMENTS

INSTITUTION	Comp	Lit	Lang	Gov/ Hist	Econ	Math	Sci	GRADE	Tuition & Fees* (In-State/Out-of-State)	Graduation** Rate (4-Year)
Arkansas State University	●			●			●	C	$8,478 / $14,778	29%
Arkansas Tech University	●	●		●		●	●	B	$7,104 / $12,528	24%
Harding University	●	●		●		●	●	B	$19,385	46%
Henderson State University	●	●		●		●	●	B	$8,530 / $10,180	16%
Hendrix College							●	F	$44,070	67%
Lyon College	●	●		●		●	●	B	$27,340	48%
Philander Smith College	●	●				●		B	$12,714	17%
Southern Arkansas University	●	●		●		●	●	B	$8,346 / $12,156	25%
University of Arkansas–Fayetteville				●		●	●	C	$9,062 / $24,308	42%
University of Arkansas–Fort Smith	●			●		●		B	$5,577 / $12,650	16%
University of Arkansas–Little Rock	●			●		●	●	B	$8,998 / $21,208	14%
University of Arkansas–Monticello	●	●		●		●	●	B	$7,462 / $13,312	12%
University of Arkansas–Pine Bluff	●	●		●		●	●	B	$7,408 / $13,738	9%
University of Central Arkansas	●			●		●	●	B	$8,524 / $15,047	23%

*   2017–18 tuition and fees. Source: U.S. Department of Education's Integrated Postsecondary Education Data System (IPEDS).
** Four-year graduation rates for first-time, full-time freshmen who enrolled in Fall 2011. Source: College Navigator.

GENERAL EDUCATION REQUIREMENTS

INSTITUTION	Comp	Lit	Lang	Gov/ Hist	Econ	Math	Sci	GRADE	Tuition & Fees* (In-State/Out-of-State)	Graduation** Rate (4-Year)
Azusa Pacific University	●						●	D	$37,506	52%
Biola University	●	●		●		●	●	B	$38,448	55%
California Baptist University	●					●	●	C	$32,256	41%
California Lutheran University	●						●	D	$41,363	62%
California Polytechnic State Univ.–San Luis Obispo	●	●		●	●	●	●	A	$9,432 / $21,312	45%
California State Polytechnic University–Pomona				●		●	●	C	$7,339 / $19,219	18%
California State University–Bakersfield	●			●		●	●	B	$7,147 / $19,027	14%
California State University–Channel Islands	●			●			●	C	$6,817 / $18,697	26%
California State University–Chico	●			●			●	C	$7,348 / $19,228	26%
California State University–Dominguez Hills	●			●		●	●	B	$6,837 / $18,717	6%
California State University–East Bay	●			●			●	C	$6,834 / $18,714	10%
California State University–Fresno	●			●		●	●	B	$6,585 / $18,465	15%
California State University–Fullerton	●			●		●	●	B	$6,850 / $18,730	22%
California State University–Long Beach	●			●		●	●	B	$6,730 / $18,610	16%
California State University–Los Angeles	●			●		●	●	B	$6,639 / $18,519	6%

* *2017–18 tuition and fees. Source: U.S. Department of Education's Integrated Postsecondary Education Data System (IPEDS).*
** *Four-year graduation rates for first-time, full-time freshmen who enrolled in Fall 2011. Source: College Navigator.*

GENERAL EDUCATION REQUIREMENTS

INSTITUTION	Comp	Lit	Lang	Gov/ Hist	Econ	Math	Sci	GRADE	Tuition & Fees (In-State/Out-of-State)	Graduation Rate (4-Year)
California State University–Monterey Bay			●			●	●	C	$7,043 / $18,923	23%
California State University–Northridge	●			●		●	●	B	$6,875 / $18,755	13%
California State University–Sacramento	●			●		●	●	B	$7,204 / $19,084	9%
California State University–San Bernardino	●	●		●		●	●	B	$6,885 / $18,765	12%
California State University–San Marcos	●		●	●		●	●	B	$7,653 / $19,533	14%
California State University–Stanislaus	●			●			●	C	$7,038 / $18,918	11%
Chapman University			●			●	●	C	$50,594	69%
Claremont McKenna College	●		●	◑	◑	●	●	B	$52,825	84%
Concordia University Irvine	●	●		●		●	●	B	$34,100	56%
Dominican University of California	●					●	●	C	$44,690	62%
Harvey Mudd College	●					●	●	C	$54,636	86%
Humboldt State University	●			●		●	●	B	$7,493 / $19,373	14%
John Paul the Great Catholic University				●		●	●	C	$24,900	61%
Loyola Marymount University	●					●		D	$46,386	70%
Mills College	●						●	D	$46,236	63%
Mount Saint Mary's University	●							F	$39,608	46%

GENERAL EDUCATION REQUIREMENTS

INSTITUTION	Comp	Lit	Lang	Gov/Hist	Econ	Math	Sci	GRADE	Tuition & Fees (In-State/Out-of-State)	Graduation Rate (4-Year)
National University	●					●	●	C	$13,016	20%
Occidental College	●						●	D	$52,838	80%
Pepperdine University	●	●	●	●		●	●	A	$51,992	77%
Pitzer College	●							F	$52,236	76%
Point Loma Nazarene University	●	●				●	●	B	$34,600	64%
Pomona College			●			●	●	C	$51,075	89%
Saint Mary's College of California	●	●	●			●	●	B	$45,686	65%
San Diego State University	●			●		●	●	B	$7,460 / $19,340	36%
San Francisco State University	●			●		●	●	B	$7,254 / $19,134	18%
San Jose State University	●			●		●	●	B	$7,721 / $19,601	10%
Santa Clara University	●					●	●	C	$49,858	85%
Scripps College	●		●			●	●	B	$52,966	83%
Soka University of America	●		●	●		●	●	B	$31,776	87%
Sonoma State University	●			●		●	●	B	$7,724 / $19,604	29%
Stanford University	●						●	D	$49,617	75%
The Master's University		●		●	●	●	●	B	$33,020	45%

GENERAL EDUCATION REQUIREMENTS

INSTITUTION	Comp	Lit	Lang	Gov/ Hist	Econ	Math	Sci	GRADE	Tuition & Fees (In-State/Out-of-State)	Graduation Rate (4-Year)
Thomas Aquinas College	●	●	●	●	●	●	●	A	$24,500	73%
University of California–Berkeley	●							F	$14,170 / $42,184	76%
University of California–Davis	◐	◐						F	$14,419 / $42,433	58%
University of California–Irvine	●					◐	◐	D	$13,738 / $41,752	70%
University of California–Los Angeles	●							F	$13,261 / $41,275	75%
University of California–Merced	●					●		D	$13,598 / $41,612	33%
University of California–Riverside	●						●	D	$13,917 / $41,931	53%
University of California–San Diego Earl Warren College	●					◐	◐	D	$14,018 / $42,032	55%
Eleanor Roosevelt College			●				●	D	$14,018 / $42,032	55%
John Muir College	●					◐	◐	D	$14,018 / $42,032	55%
Revelle College	●	●	●			●	●	B	$14,018 / $42,032	55%
Sixth College	●					●	●	C	$14,018 / $42,032	55%
Thurgood Marshall College	●			●		●	●	B	$14,018 / $42,032	55%
University of California–Santa Barbara	●					◐	◐	D	$14,451 / $42,465	68%
University of California–Santa Cruz	●					◐	◐	D	$14,020 / $42,034	53%

GENERAL EDUCATION REQUIREMENTS

INSTITUTION	Comp	Lit	Lang	Gov/ Hist	Econ	Math	Sci	GRADE	Tuition & Fees (In-State/Out-of-State)	Graduation Rate (4-Year)
University of La Verne	●						●	D	$41,450	52%
University of Redlands						●	●	D	$48,072	71%
University of Saint Katherine	●	●		●	●	●	●	A	$23,500	70%
University of San Diego	●	●	●			●	●	B	$47,708	69%
University of San Francisco						●	●	D	$46,250	67%
University of Southern California	●		●				●	C	$54,259	77%
University of the Pacific						●	●	D	$46,346	47%
Vanguard University of Southern California	●	●		●			●	B	$32,430	57%
Westmont College		●					●	D	$44,044	67%
Whittier College	●							F	$46,310	62%

COLORADO

GENERAL EDUCATION REQUIREMENTS

INSTITUTION	Comp	Lit	Lang	Gov/Hist	Econ	Math	Sci	GRADE	Tuition & Fees* (In-State/Out-of-State)	Graduation** Rate (4-Year)
Adams State University	●					●	●	C	$9,440 / $20,456	14%
Colorado Christian University	●	●		●	●	●	●	A	$30,370	41%
Colorado College							●	F	$52,818	82%
Colorado Mesa University	●					●	●	C	$8,374 / $20,330	21%
Colorado State University–Fort Collins	●					●	●	C	$11,395 / $28,903	45%
Colorado State University–Pueblo	●					●	●	C	$10,090 / $25,547	19%
Fort Lewis College	●						●	D	$8,609 / $18,761	21%
Metropolitan State University of Denver	●					●	●	C	$7,352 / $20,149	8%
Regis University	●	●			●		●	B	$35,610	60%
United States Air Force Academy	●	●		●	●	●	●	A	$0	75%
University of Colorado–Boulder	●		●				●	C	$12,086 / $36,220	45%
University of Colorado–Colorado Springs	●							F	$8,314 / $19,498	23%
University of Colorado–Denver	●					●	●	C	$9,107 / $25,259	23%
University of Denver	●						●	D	$48,669	65%

* 2017–18 tuition and fees. Source: U.S. Department of Education's Integrated Postsecondary Education Data System (IPEDS).
** Four-year graduation rates for first-time, full-time freshmen who enrolled in Fall 2011. Source: College Navigator.

GENERAL EDUCATION REQUIREMENTS

INSTITUTION	Comp	Lit	Lang	Gov/Hist	Econ	Math	Sci	GRADE	Tuition & Fees (In-State/Out-of-State)	Graduation Rate (4-Year)
University of Northern Colorado							●	F	$9,546 / $21,132	28%
Western State Colorado University	●						●	D	$9,802 / $21,274	21%

CONNECTICUT

GENERAL EDUCATION REQUIREMENTS

INSTITUTION	Comp	Lit	Lang	Gov/ Hist	Econ	Math	Sci	GRADE	Tuition & Fees* (In-State/Out-of-State)	Graduation** Rate (4-Year)
Central Connecticut State University	●	●				●	●	B	$10,225 / $22,914	24%
Connecticut College	●						●	D	$52,850	80%
Eastern Connecticut State University	●					●	●	C	$10,919 / $23,608	41%
Fairfield University	●	●	●			●	●	B	$47,165	79%
Quinnipiac University	●					●		D	$46,780	71%
Sacred Heart University		●				●		D	$39,820	67%
Southern Connecticut State University	●		●			●	●	B	$10,538 / $23,226	20%
Trinity College							●	F	$54,770	77%
United States Coast Guard Academy	●			●	●	●	●	B	$0	77%
University of Bridgeport	●					●	●	C	$32,250	32%
University of Connecticut	●		●			●	●	B	$14,880 / $36,948	70%
University of Hartford						●	●	D	$38,910	1%
University of New Haven							●	F	$38,170	52%
Wesleyan University								F	$52,804	85%

* *2017–18 tuition and fees. Source: U.S. Department of Education's Integrated Postsecondary Education Data System (IPEDS).*
** *Four-year graduation rates for first-time, full-time freshmen who enrolled in Fall 2011. Source: College Navigator.*

CONNECTICUT (continued)

GENERAL EDUCATION REQUIREMENTS

INSTITUTION	Comp	Lit	Lang	Gov/Hist	Econ	Math	Sci	GRADE	Tuition & Fees (In-State/Out-of-State)	Graduation Rate (4-Year)
Western Connecticut State University							●	F	$10,418 / $23,107	20%
Yale University	●		●				●	C	$51,400	87%

DELAWARE

GENERAL EDUCATION REQUIREMENTS

INSTITUTION	Comp	Lit	Lang	Gov/ Hist	Econ	Math	Sci	GRADE	Tuition & Fees* (In-State/Out-of-State)	Graduation** Rate (4-Year)
Delaware State University	●	●					●	C	$7,868 / $16,904	19%
University of Delaware	●					●	●	C	$13,160 / $33,150	73%
Wesley College	●	●				●	●	B	$26,406	7%
Wilmington University	●				●	●	●	B	$10,940	17%

*   2017–18 tuition and fees. Source: U.S. Department of Education's Integrated Postsecondary Education Data System (IPEDS).
** Four-year graduation rates for first-time, full-time freshmen who enrolled in Fall 2011. Source: College Navigator.

GENERAL EDUCATION REQUIREMENTS

INSTITUTION	Comp	Lit	Lang	Gov/Hist	Econ	Math	Sci	GRADE	Tuition & Fees* (In-State/Out-of-State)	Graduation** Rate (4-Year)
American University	●					●	●	C	$46,615	76%
Catholic University of America	●		●			●		C	$44,060	66%
Gallaudet University	●		●			●		C	$16,558	24%
Georgetown University	●		●			◐	◐	C	$52,300	90%
Howard University	●		●			●		C	$25,697	43%
The George Washington University	●					●	●	C	$53,518	73%
University of the District of Columbia	●					●	●	C	$5,756 / $12,092	18%

* *2017–18 tuition and fees. Source: U.S. Department of Education's Integrated Postsecondary Education Data System (IPEDS).*
** *Four-year graduation rates for first-time, full-time freshmen who enrolled in Fall 2011. Source: College Navigator.*

FLORIDA

GENERAL EDUCATION REQUIREMENTS

INSTITUTION	Comp	Lit	Lang	Gov/Hist	Econ	Math	Sci	GRADE	Tuition & Fees* (In-State/Out-of-State)	Graduation** Rate (4-Year)
Ave Maria University	●			●		●	●	B	$19,970	46%
Barry University	●			●		●	●	B	$29,850	15%
Bethune-Cookman University	●	●		●		●	●	B	$14,410	13%
Eckerd College	●	●				●		C	$43,044	63%
Flagler College	●	●				●	●	B	$18,200	43%
Florida A&M University	●			●		●	●	B	$5,785 / $17,725	13%
Florida Atlantic University	●					●	●	C	$4,831 / $17,276	24%
Florida Gulf Coast University	●					●	●	C	$6,118 / $25,162	22%
Florida International University	●					●	●	C	$6,556 / $18,954	27%
Florida Southern College	●						●	D	$34,774	57%
Florida State University	●		●			●	●	B	$5,656 / $18,786	63%
Jacksonville University	●	●			●	●	●	B	$35,260	32%
Lynn University						●	●	D	$37,510	45%
New College of Florida								F	$6,916 / $29,944	57%
Nova Southeastern University	●					●		D	$29,930 / $29,930	41%

* 2017–18 tuition and fees. Source: U.S. Department of Education's Integrated Postsecondary Education Data System (IPEDS).
** Four-year graduation rates for first-time, full-time freshmen who enrolled in Fall 2011. Source: College Navigator.

GENERAL EDUCATION REQUIREMENTS

INSTITUTION	Comp	Lit	Lang	Gov/Hist	Econ	Math	Sci	GRADE	Tuition & Fees (In-State/Out-of-State)	Graduation Rate (4-Year)
Palm Beach Atlantic University	●	●		●		●		B	$29,950	43%
Rollins College	●		●					D	$48,335	68%
Saint Leo University	●	●					●	C	$22,220	34%
Southeastern University	●	●				●	●	B	$25,360	24%
Stetson University	●							F	$44,490	55%
University of Central Florida	●			◒	◒	●	●	B	$6,368 / $22,467	40%
University of Florida	●					●	●	C	$6,381 / $28,659	68%
University of Miami	●		●			●	●	B	$48,484	72%
University of North Florida	●	●				●	●	B	$6,394 / $20,798	30%
University of South Florida	●					●	●	C	$6,410 / $17,324	51%
University of Tampa	●					●	●	C	$28,426	49%
University of West Florida	●					●	●	C	$6,360 / $19,241	22%

GEORGIA

GENERAL EDUCATION REQUIREMENTS

INSTITUTION	Comp	Lit	Lang	Gov/ Hist	Econ	Math	Sci	GRADE	Tuition & Fees* (In-State/Out-of-State)	Graduation** Rate (4-Year)
Agnes Scott College	●		●			◐	◐	C	$39,960	65%
Albany State University	●	●		●		●	●	B	$5,675 / $16,136	8%
Armstrong State University	●	●		●			●	B	$5,439 / $15,900	13%
Augusta University	●	●		●			●	B	$8,604 / $23,606	7%
Berry College	●					●	●	C	$35,176	57%
Clark Atlanta University	●					◐	◐	D	$21,892	26%
Clayton State University	●	●		●		●	●	B	$5,419 / $15,880	11%
Columbus State University	●			●			●	C	$6,134 / $16,920	12%
Dalton State College	●	●		●				B	$4,212 / $12,634	9%
Emory University	◐	◐				●	●	C	$49,392	82%
Fort Valley State University	●	●		●		●	●	B	$6,658 / $19,738	7%
Georgia College & State University	●	●		●			●	B	$9,346 / $28,060	50%
Georgia Gwinnett College	●			●		●	●	B	$5,634 / $16,348	3%
Georgia Institute of Technology	●			●		●	●	B	$12,418 / $33,014	39%

* 2017–18 tuition and fees. Source: U.S. Department of Education's Integrated Postsecondary Education Data System (IPEDS).
** Four-year graduation rates for first-time, full-time freshmen who enrolled in Fall 2011. Source: College Navigator.

GENERAL EDUCATION REQUIREMENTS

INSTITUTION	Comp	Lit	Lang	Gov/Hist	Econ	Math	Sci	GRADE	Tuition & Fees (In State/Out of State)	Graduation Rate (4-Year)
Georgia Southern University	●	●		●	●	●	●	A	$6,356 / $17,142	26%
Georgia Southwestern State University	●	●		●		●	●	B	$5,341 / $15,802	11%
Georgia State University	●			●		●	●	B	$9,112 / $23,971	24%
Kennesaw State University	●	●		●	●	●	●	A	$6,347 / $17,329	13%
Mercer University	●					●	●	C	$36,000	47%
Middle Georgia State University	●	●		●			●	B	$3,924 / $11,092	N/A
Morehouse College	●	●	●	●		●	●	A	$27,278	42%
Oglethorpe University		●				●	●	C	$36,680	38%
Paine College	●	●		●		●	●	B	$14,226	11%
Savannah State University	●			●		●	●	B	$5,743 / $16,204	9%
Spelman College	●		●				●	C	$28,181	69%
University of Georgia	●	●	●	●		●	●	A	$11,818 / $30,392	62%
University of North Georgia	●			●			●	C	$4,421 / $12,834	28%
University of West Georgia	●			●			●	C	$6,226 / $17,010	15%
Valdosta State University	●	●		●		●	●	B	$6,410 / $17,196	16%

HAWAII

GENERAL EDUCATION REQUIREMENTS

INSTITUTION	Comp	Lit	Lang	Gov/ Hist	Econ	Math	Sci	GRADE	Tuition & Fees* (In-State/Out-of-State)	Graduation** Rate (4-Year)
Brigham Young University–Hawaii	●							F	$5,400	22%
Chaminade University	●	●					●	C	$24,514	38%
Hawaii Pacific University	●						●	D	$24,550	23%
University of Hawaii–Hilo	●					●	●	C	$7,648 / $20,608	14%
University of Hawaii–Manoa	●		●			●	●	B	$11,754 / $33,786	28%
University of Hawaii–West Oahu	●					●	●	C	$7,440 / $20,400	17%

* 2017–18 tuition and fees. Source: U.S. Department of Education's Integrated Postsecondary Education Data System (IPEDS).
** Four-year graduation rates for first-time, full-time freshmen who enrolled in Fall 2011. Source: College Navigator.

IDAHO

GENERAL EDUCATION REQUIREMENTS

INSTITUTION	Comp	Lit	Lang	Gov/ Hist	Econ	Math	Sci	GRADE	Tuition & Fees* (In-State/Out-of-State)	Graduation** Rate (4-Year)
Boise State University						●	●	D	$7,326 / $22,642	19%
Brigham Young University–Idaho	●						●	D	$4,018	19%
Idaho State University	●						●	D	$7,166 / $21,942	13%
Lewis-Clark State College		●				●	●	C	$6,334 / $18,410	9%
Northwest Nazarene University	●			●			●	C	$29,000	36%
The College of Idaho						●	●	D	$28,755	59%
University of Idaho						●	●	D	$7,488 / $23,812	30%

* 2017–18 tuition and fees. Source: U.S. Department of Education's Integrated Postsecondary Education Data System (IPEDS).
** Four-year graduation rates for first-time, full-time freshmen who enrolled in Fall 2011. Source: College Navigator.

ILLINOIS

GENERAL EDUCATION REQUIREMENTS

INSTITUTION	Comp	Lit	Lang	Gov/ Hist	Econ	Math	Sci	GRADE	Tuition & Fees* (In-State/Out-of-State)	Graduation** Rate (4-Year)
Augustana College	●						●	D	$40,908	70%
Aurora University	●							F	$23,520	38%
Benedictine University	●					●	●	C	$33,900	34%
Bradley University	●					●		D	$32,930	51%
Chicago State University	●					●	●	C	$10,252 / $17,212	2%
Concordia University Chicago	●	●					●	C	$31,588	45%
DePaul University	●					●		D	$39,010	59%
Dominican University	●					●	●	C	$32,530	47%
Eastern Illinois University	●						●	D	$11,678 / $13,868	33%
Elmhurst College	●						●	D	$36,370	53%
Governors State University	●					●	●	C	$11,746 / $21,136	N/A
Illinois College	●						●	D	$32,140	55%
Illinois State University	●					●	●	C	$14,061 / $25,168	47%
Illinois Wesleyan University	●		●					D	$45,856	71%
Knox College						●	●	D	$44,958	72%

*   2017–18 tuition and fees. Source: U.S. Department of Education's Integrated Postsecondary Education Data System (IPEDS).
** Four-year graduation rates for first-time, full-time freshmen who enrolled in Fall 2011. Source: College Navigator.

GENERAL EDUCATION REQUIREMENTS

INSTITUTION	Comp	Lit	Lang	Gov/Hist	Econ	Math	Sci	GRADE	Tuition & Fees (In-State/Out-of-State)	Graduation Rate (4-Year)
Lake Forest College								F	$45,548	66%
Lewis University	•				•	•	•	B	$31,250	48%
Loyola University Chicago	•	•				•	•	B	$43,078	69%
MacMurray College	•							F	$26,100	41%
McKendree University	•			◐	◐	•	•	B	$29,640	37%
Millikin University	•			•			•	C	$33,066	48%
Monmouth College	•							F	$36,400	51%
National Louis University	•						•	D	$10,440	25%
North Central College	•					•	•	C	$37,749	61%
North Park University						•	•	D	$28,620	40%
Northeastern Illinois University	•						•	D	$10,736 / $19,792	4%
Northern Illinois University	•							F	$14,350 / $23,816	21%
Northwestern University			•				•	D	$52,678	84%
Olivet Nazarene University	•	•				•	•	B	$34,940	55%
Principia College						•	•	D	$28,920	71%
Quincy University	•	•				•	•	B	$27,770	35%

GENERAL EDUCATION REQUIREMENTS

INSTITUTION	Comp	Lit	Lang	Gov/ Hist	Econ	Math	Sci	GRADE	Tuition & Fees (In-State/Out-of-State)	Graduation Rate (4-Year)
Rockford University	●						●	D	$30,050	39%
Roosevelt University	●	●					●	C	$28,963	31%
Saint Xavier University	●					●	●	C	$33,380	34%
Southern Illinois University–Carbondale	●					●	●	C	$13,932 / $28,107	23%
Southern Illinois University–Edwardsville	●					●	●	C	$11,493 / $24,651	27%
University of Chicago	●	●				●	●	B	$56,034	88%
University of Illinois–Chicago	●		●			●	●	B	$13,704 / $26,560	30%
University of Illinois–Springfield	●					●	●	C	$11,413 / $20,938	36%
University of Illinois–Urbana-Champaign			●					F	$15,074 / $31,194	70%
University of St. Francis	●	●				●	●	B	$31,470	41%
Western Illinois University	●					●	●	C	$12,897 / $12,897	30%
Wheaton College	●	●	●				●	B	$35,190	80%

INDIANA

GENERAL EDUCATION REQUIREMENTS

INSTITUTION	Comp	Lit	Lang	Gov/ Hist	Econ	Math	Sci	GRADE	Tuition & Fees* (In-State/Out-of-State)	Graduation** Rate (4-Year)
Anderson University	●						●	D	$29,710	48%
Ball State University	●					●		D	$9,774 / $25,942	48%
Butler University			●			●	●	C	$39,860	63%
DePauw University						◐	◐	F	$47,838	76%
Earlham College							●	F	$45,750	58%
Goshen College	●						●	D	$33,200	62%
Hanover College						●	●	D	$36,520	69%
Indiana State University	●	●					●	C	$8,916 / $19,452	23%
Indiana University-Bloomington	●					●	●	C	$10,533 / $34,845	63%
Indiana University-East	●					●	●	C	$7,207 / $19,038	17%
Indiana University-Kokomo						●	●	C	$7,207 / $19,038	18%
Indiana Universityy-Northwest							●	F	$7,207 / $19,038	9%
Indiana University–Purdue University Fort Wayne							●	F	$8,330 / $20,005	11%
Indiana University–Purdue University Indianapolis	●					●	●	C	$9,334 / $29,806	21%
Indiana University–South Bend	●					●	●	C	$7,207 / $19,038	9%

* 2017–18 tuition and fees. Source: U.S. Department of Education's Integrated Postsecondary Education Data System (IPEDS).
** Four-year graduation rates for first-time, full-time freshmen who enrolled in Fall 2011. Source: College Navigator.

GENERAL EDUCATION REQUIREMENTS

INSTITUTION	Comp	Lit	Lang	Gov/ Hist	Econ	Math	Sci	GRADE	Tuition & Fees (In-State/Out-of-State)	Graduation Rate (4-Year)
Indiana University–Southeast	●						●	D	$7,207 / $19,038	14%
Indiana Wesleyan University	●	●					●	C	$25,980	52%
Marian University	●						●	D	$33,000	34%
Oakland City University	●	●				●	●	B	$23,700	42%
Purdue University Northwest	●					●	●	C	$7,582 / $17,129	12%
Purdue University–West Lafayette	●					●	●	C	$9,992 / $28,794	51%
Saint Mary's College		●				●	●	C	$40,800	73%
Taylor University	●	●				●	●	B	$32,885	71%
University of Evansville						●	●	D	$35,394	62%
University of Indianapolis	●	●				●	●	B	$28,390	43%
University of Notre Dame			●			●	●	C	$51,505	90%
University of Saint Francis	●						●	D	$29,430	39%
University of Southern Indiana	●					●	●	C	$7,970 / $18,626	21%
Valparaiso University		●					●	D	$38,760	62%
Wabash College						●	●	D	$42,250	72%

IOWA

GENERAL EDUCATION REQUIREMENTS

INSTITUTION	Comp	Lit	Lang	Gov/ Hist	Econ	Math	Sci	GRADE	Tuition & Fees* (In-State/Out-of-State)	Graduation** Rate (4-Year)
Central College							●	F	$35,930	65%
Coe College							●	F	$42,430	61%
Cornell College			●			●	●	C	$40,880	64%
Drake University						●	●	D	$39,062	70%
Grand View University	●							F	$26,516	32%
Grinnell College								F	$50,714	84%
Iowa State University	●						●	D	$8,636 / $22,472	45%
Loras College	●					●	●	C	$32,886	57%
Luther College							●	F	$41,020	71%
Simpson College								F	$37,663	63%
St. Ambrose University	●						●	D	$30,016	52%
University of Iowa	●	●	●				●	B	$8,965 / $30,609	54%
University of Northern Iowa		●				●	●	C	$8,699 / $19,241	40%
Upper Iowa University	●					●	●	C	$29,600	31%
Wartburg College	●						●	D	$39,730	60%

* 2017–18 tuition and fees. Source: U.S. Department of Education's Integrated Postsecondary Education Data System (IPEDS).
** Four-year graduation rates for first-time, full-time freshmen who enrolled in Fall 2011. Source: College Navigator.

KANSAS

GENERAL EDUCATION REQUIREMENTS

INSTITUTION	Comp	Lit	Lang	Gov/Hist	Econ	Math	Sci	GRADE	Tuition & Fees* (In-State/Out-of-State)	Graduation** Rate (4-Year)
Baker University						●	●	D	$28,960	41%
Benedictine College	●						●	D	$28,480	46%
Bethel College	●						●	D	$27,720	31%
Emporia State University	●					●	●	C	$6,345 / $19,918	26%
Fort Hays State University	●					●	●	C	$5,009 / $14,832	21%
Kansas State University	●					●	●	C	$10,135 / $25,492	33%
Pittsburg State University	●						●	D	$7,100 / $18,152	24%
University of Kansas							●	F	$10,824 / $26,592	42%
Washburn University	●					●	●	C	$7,978 / $17,918	16%
Wichita State University	●			●			●	C	$8,432 / $17,390	22%

* *2017–18 tuition and fees. Source: U.S. Department of Education's Integrated Postsecondary Education Data System (IPEDS).*
** *Four-year graduation rates for first-time, full-time freshmen who enrolled in Fall 2011. Source: College Navigator.*

GENERAL EDUCATION REQUIREMENTS

INSTITUTION	Comp	Lit	Lang	Gov/ Hist	Econ	Math	Sci	GRADE	Tuition & Fees* (In-State/Out-of-State)	Graduation** Rate (4-Year)
Alice Lloyd College	●	●					●	C	$11,550	90%
Asbury University	●	●	●				●	B	$29,500	57%
Bellarmine University	●						●	D	$40,750	50%
Berea College	●						●	D	$25,760†	49%
Centre College	●	●	◐			◐	●	B	$40,500	80%
Eastern Kentucky University	●					●	●	C	$9,366 / $18,250	29%
Georgetown College	●	●	●				●	B	$37,160	45%
Kentucky State University	●						●	D	$8,184 / $19,638	9%
Lindsey Wilson College	●						●	D	$24,246	20%
Morehead State University	●					◐	◐	D	$8,950 / $13,426	23%
Murray State University	●	●				●	●	B	$8,820 / $23,820	28%
Northern Kentucky University	●					●	●	C	$9,744 / $19,104	15%
Transylvania University	●					●		D	$37,290	69%
University of Kentucky	●					●	●	C	$11,942 / $28,046	40%

* 2017–18 tuition and fees. Source: U.S. Department of Education's Integrated Postsecondary Education Data System (IPEDS).

** Four-year graduation rates for first-time, full-time freshmen who enrolled in Fall 2011. Source: College Navigator.

† Berea College grants full-tuition scholarships to all admitted students.

KENTUCKY (continued)

GENERAL EDUCATION REQUIREMENTS

INSTITUTION	Comp	Lit	Lang	Gov/Hist	Econ	Math	Sci	GRADE	Tuition & Fees (In-State/Out-of-State)	Graduation Rate (4-Year)
University of Louisville	•					•	•	C	$11,264 / $26,286	31%
University of Pikeville	•					•	•	C	$20,338	17%
University of the Cumberlands	•	•						D	$23,000	29%
Western Kentucky University		•					•	D	$10,202 / $25,512	28%

GENERAL EDUCATION REQUIREMENTS

INSTITUTION	Comp	Lit	Lang	Gov/ Hist	Econ	Math	Sci	GRADE	Tuition & Fees* (In-State/Out-of-State)	Graduation** Rate (4-Year)
Centenary College						•	•	D	$35,900	43%
Dillard University	•	•			•	•	•	B	$17,917	26%
Grambling State University	•	•			•	•	•	B	$7,435 / $16,733	13%
Louisiana College	•	•					•	C	$16,000	25%
Louisiana State University–Alexandria						•	•	D	$6,669 / $14,024	4%
Louisiana State University–Baton Rouge						•	•	D	$11,374 / $28,051	38%
Louisiana State University–Shreveport							•	F	$7,166 / $20,320	13%
Louisiana Tech University	•					•	•	C	$9,645 / $18,558	32%
Loyola University New Orleans	•						•	D	$39,492	47%
McNeese State University		•				•	•	C	$7,920 / $15,958	31%
Nicholls State University							•	F	$7,886 / $8,979	26%
Northwestern State University of Louisiana		•					•	D	$7,922 / $18,710	23%
Southeastern Louisiana University	•	•				•	•	B	$8,153 / $20,631	18%
Southern University–New Orleans	•	•		•		•	•	B	$6,421 / $15,322	5%

* *2017–18 tuition and fees. Source: U.S. Department of Education's Integrated Postsecondary Education Data System (IPEDS).*
** *Four-year graduation rates for first-time, full-time freshmen who enrolled in Fall 2011. Source: College Navigator.*

GENERAL EDUCATION REQUIREMENTS

INSTITUTION	Comp	Lit	Lang	Gov/ Hist	Econ	Math	Sci	GRADE	Tuition & Fees (In-State/Out-of-State)	Graduation Rate (4-Year)
Southern University and A&M College	●	●				●	●	B	$8,666 / $18,080	8%
Tulane University	●					●	●	C	$52,960	73%
University of Louisiana–Lafayette	●	●				●	●	B	$9,888 / $23,616	15%
University of Louisiana–Monroe		●				●	●	C	$8,470 / $20,570	20%
University of New Orleans	●	●				●	●	B	$8,484 / $13,320	14%
Xavier University of Louisiana	●	●				●	●	B	$23,606	30%

MAINE

GENERAL EDUCATION REQUIREMENTS

INSTITUTION	Comp	Lit	Lang	Gov/ Hist	Econ	Math	Sci	GRADE	Tuition & Fees* (In-State/Out-of-State)	Graduation** Rate (4-Year)
Bates College	●						●	D	$52,042	89%
Bowdoin College							●	F	$51,848	91%
Colby College	●	●	●			●	●	B	$53,120	89%
College of the Atlantic						◐	◐	F	$43,542	53%
Husson University	●	●				●		C	$17,561	31%
University of Maine–Augusta	●						●	D	$7,808 / $17,498	6%
University of Maine–Farmington	●						●	D	$9,458 / $19,026	35%
University of Maine–Fort Kent	●	●				●	●	B	$7,965 / $12,075	17%
University of Maine–Machias	●	●					●	C	$7,680 / $19,320	19%
University of Maine–Orono	●						●	D	$10,902 / $30,282	38%
University of Maine–Presque Isle	●						●	D	$7,885 / $11,995	15%
University of New England	●					●	●	C	$36,530	54%
University of Southern Maine	●						●	D	$8,638 / $20,594	15%

* 2017–18 tuition and fees. Source: U.S. Department of Education's Integrated Postsecondary Education Data System (IPEDS).
** Four-year graduation rates for first-time, full-time freshmen who enrolled in Fall 2011. Source: College Navigator.

MARYLAND

GENERAL EDUCATION REQUIREMENTS

INSTITUTION	Comp	Lit	Lang	Gov/Hist	Econ	Math	Sci	GRADE	Tuition & Fees* (In-State/Out-of-State)	Graduation** Rate (4-Year)
Bowie State University	●			●		●	●	B	$8,064 / $18,653	15%
Coppin State University	●	◑		◑		●	●	B	$7,474 / $13,622	10%
Frostburg State University	●						●	D	$8,914 / $22,262	26%
Goucher College	●					●		D	$43,440	56%
Hood College	●	●					●	C	$37,960	54%
Johns Hopkins University								F	$52,170	87%
Loyola University Maryland	●	●	●				●	B	$47,560	77%
McDaniel College						●		F	$41,800	58%
Morgan State University	●					●	●	C	$7,766 / $17,832	13%
Mount St. Mary's University	●	●		●		●	●	B	$40,550	58%
Notre Dame of Maryland University	●	●					●	C	$36,070	38%
Salisbury University	●					●	●	C	$9,582 / $18,622	49%
St. John's College		●	●	●	●	●	●	A	$51,795	63%
St. Mary's College of Maryland						●	●	D	$14,496 / $29,948	70%

*   2017–18 tuition and fees. Source: U.S. Department of Education's Integrated Postsecondary Education Data System (IPEDS).
** Four-year graduation rates for first-time, full-time freshmen who enrolled in Fall 2011. Source: College Navigator.

GENERAL EDUCATION REQUIREMENTS

INSTITUTION	Comp	Lit	Lang	Gov/Hist	Econ	Math	Sci	GRADE	Tuition & Fees (In-State/Out-of-State)	Graduation Rate (4-Year)
Stevenson University	●	●					●	C	$35,490	41%
Towson University	●						●	D	$9,694 / $22,140	47%
United States Naval Academy	●	●		●		●	●	B	$0	90%
University of Baltimore	●					●	●	C	$8,824 / $20,704	9%
University of Maryland–Baltimore County	●		●			●	●	B	$11,518 / $25,654	39%
University of Maryland–College Park	●					●	●	C	$10,399 / $33,606	67%
University of Maryland–Eastern Shore	●					●	●	C	$8,042 / $18,048	20%
Washington College	●						●	D	$44,820	73%

MASSACHUSETTS

GENERAL EDUCATION REQUIREMENTS

INSTITUTION	Comp	Lit	Lang	Gov/ Hist	Econ	Math	Sci	GRADE	Tuition & Fees* (In-State/Out-of-State)	Graduation** Rate (4-Year)
Amherst College								F	$54,310	90%
Assumption College	●	●				●	●	B	$39,598	68%
Bay Path University	●	●					●	C	$33,557	53%
Bentley University	●				●	●	●	B	$48,000	87%
Boston College	●	●	●				●	B	$53,346	88%
Boston University	●		●					D	$52,082	81%
Brandeis University	●		●					D	$53,537	83%
Bridgewater State University						●	●	C	$10,012 / $16,152	33%
Clark University							●	F	$44,400	77%
College of the Holy Cross		●					●	D	$50,630	91%
Curry College	●						●	D	$38,936	45%
Emerson College	●	●					●	C	$44,832	77%
Endicott College	●							F	$32,154	71%
Fitchburg State University	●						●	D	$10,155 / $16,235	36%
Framingham State University	●					●	●	C	$9,920 / $16,000	35%

* *2017–18 tuition and fees. Source: U.S. Department of Education's Integrated Postsecondary Education Data System (IPEDS).*
** *Four-year graduation rates for first-time, full-time freshmen who enrolled in Fall 2011. Source: College Navigator.*

GENERAL EDUCATION REQUIREMENTS

INSTITUTION	Comp	Lit	Lang	Gov/Hist	Econ	Math	Sci	GRADE	Tuition & Fees (In-State/Out-of-State)	Graduation Rate (4-Year)
Gordon College	●	●				◐	◐	C	$36,740	61%
Hampshire College								F	$51,608	47%
Harvard University	●						●	D	$48,949	84%
Lesley University	●	●				●		C	$26,675	49%
Massachusetts College of Liberal Arts	●					●	●	C	$10,135 / $19,080	40%
Merrimack College	●					◐	◐	D	$40,190	63%
Mount Holyoke College							●	F	$47,940	81%
Northeastern University	●							F	$49,497	N/A
Salem State University						●	●	D	$10,278 / $16,706	29%
Simmons College	●						●	D	$39,600	67%
Smith College								F	$50,044	82%
Springfield College	●						●	D	$36,535	68%
Stonehill College								F	$41,300	77%
Suffolk University	●					●	●	C	$37,270	45%
Tufts University	●		●			●	●	B	$54,318	87%
University of Massachusetts–Amherst	●						●	D	$15,411 / $33,477	67%

GENERAL EDUCATION REQUIREMENTS

INSTITUTION	Comp	Lit	Lang	Gov/ Hist	Econ	Math	Sci	GRADE	Tuition & Fees (In-State/Out-of-State)	Graduation Rate (4-Year)
University of Massachusetts–Boston	●					●	●	C	$13,828 / $32,985	21%
University of Massachusetts–Dartmouth	●	●				●	●	B	$13,571 / $28,285	30%
University of Massachusetts–Lowell	●						●	D	$14,800 / $31,865	39%
Wellesley College	●		●			●	●	B	$51,148	81%
Western New England University	●	●				●	●	B	$35,740	53%
Westfield State University	●			●		●	●	B	$9,715 / $15,795	53%
Wheaton College	●						●	D	$50,850	74%
Williams College	●					◐	◐	D	$53,550	86%
Worcester State University	●						●	D	$9,532 / $15,612	36%

GENERAL EDUCATION REQUIREMENTS

INSTITUTION	Comp	Lit	Lang	Gov/Hist	Econ	Math	Sci	GRADE	Tuition & Fees* (In-State/Out-of-State)	Graduation** Rate (4-Year)
Albion College	●							F	$43,050	46%
Alma College	●						●	D	$38,768	56%
Andrews University	●					●	●	C	$28,436	33%
Aquinas College	●					●	●	C	$31,244	36%
Calvin College	●	●	●			●	●	B	$33,100	59%
Central Michigan University	●						●	D	$12,510 / $23,670	24%
Cornerstone University	●						●	D	$27,520	37%
Eastern Michigan University							●	F	$12,019 / $29,200	14%
Ferris State University	●						●	D	$11,628 / $18,588	22%
Grand Valley State University	●					●		D	$11,994 / $17,064	36%
Hillsdale College	●	●		●		●	●	B	$26,742	71%
Hope College	●	●					●	C	$32,780	67%
Kalamazoo College	●							F	$46,840	82%
Lake Superior State University	●						●	D	$11,427 / $11,427	34%

*   2017–18 tuition and fees. Source: U.S. Department of Education's Integrated Postsecondary Education Data System (IPEDS).
** Four-year graduation rates for first-time, full-time freshmen who enrolled in Fall 2011. Source: College Navigator.

GENERAL EDUCATION REQUIREMENTS

INSTITUTION	Comp	Lit	Lang	Gov/Hist	Econ	Math	Sci	GRADE	Tuition & Fees (In-State/Out-of-State)	Graduation Rate (4-Year)
Lawrence Technological University	●	●		●		●	●	B	$32,190	18%
Madonna University	●	●				●	●	B	$20,700	37%
Michigan State University	●					●	●	C	$14,460 / $39,406	52%
Michigan Technological University	●					●	●	C	$15,074 / $32,318	28%
Northern Michigan University	●						●	D	$10,240 / $15,736	25%
Oakland University	●						●	D	$11,970 / $23,873	19%
Olivet College	●					●		D	$26,695	38%
Saginaw Valley State University	●	●				●	●	B	$9,819 / $23,063	11%
Spring Arbor University	●	●				●	●	B	$27,750	38%
University of Detroit Mercy	●	●						C	$41,158	46%
University of Michigan–Ann Arbor	●		●				●	C	$14,826 / $47,476	77%
University of Michigan–Dearborn							●	F	$12,472 / $24,706	17%
University of Michigan–Flint	●						●	D	$10,842 / $21,165	15%
Wayne State University	●						●	D	$12,729 / $27,203	19%
Western Michigan University	●							F	$11,943 / $14,699	22%

GENERAL EDUCATION REQUIREMENTS

INSTITUTION	Comp	Lit	Lang	Gov/ Hist	Econ	Math	Sci	GRADE	Tuition & Fees* (In-State/Out-of-State)	Graduation** Rate (4-Year)
Augsburg University	●						●	D	$37,615	45%
Bemidji State University	●						●	D	$8,677 / $8,677	28%
Bethany Lutheran College	●	●				●	●	B	$26,830	40%
Bethel University							●	F	$36,210	62%
Carleton College	●		●			●	●	B	$52,782	89%
College of St. Benedict & St. John's University			●			●		D	$43,738 / $43,356†	76%/66%†
Concordia College	●					●	●	C	$38,378	67%
Concordia University–St. Paul	●	●				●	●	B	$21,750	40%
Crown College	●	●					●	C	$25,430	52%
Gustavus Adolphus College	●					●	●	C	$44,080	77%
Hamline University	●						●	D	$40,332	59%
Macalester College	●		●					D	$52,464	85%
Metropolitan State University						●		F	$7,859 / $14,960	14%
Minnesota State University–Mankato	●					●	●	C	$8,164 / $16,216	24%

*   *2017–18 tuition and fees. Source: U.S. Department of Education's Integrated Postsecondary Education Data System (IPEDS).*
** *Four-year graduation rates for first-time, full-time freshmen who enrolled in Fall 2011. Source: College Navigator.*
†   *The College of St. Benedict and St. John's University share an academic program but have separate tuition & fees and graduation rates.*

GENERAL EDUCATION REQUIREMENTS

INSTITUTION	Comp	Lit	Lang	Gov/ Hist	Econ	Math	Sci	GRADE	Tuition & Fees (In-State/Out-of-State)	Graduation Rate (4-Year)
Minnesota State University–Moorhead	●					●	●	C	$8,468 / $15,878	26%
Saint Mary's University of Minnesota	●	●				●	●	B	$33,560	54%
Southwest Minnesota State University	●					●	●	C	$8,610	28%
St. Catherine University						●	●	D	$38,170	37%
St. Cloud State University							●	F	$8,228 / $16,462	19%
St. Olaf College	●		●			●	●	B	$46,000	85%
The College of St. Scholastica	●	●					●	C	$36,212	58%
University of Minnesota–Crookston	●					●	●	C	$11,814 / N/A	41%
University of Minnesota–Duluth							●	F	$13,344 / $18,462	36%
University of Minnesota–Morris	●						●	D	$13,072 / $15,092	50%
University of Minnesota–Twin Cities	●					●	●	C	$14,417 / $26,603	64%
University of Northwestern–St. Paul	●	●					●	C	$30,794	47%
University of St. Thomas	●	●	●			●	●	B	$41,133	67%
Winona State University	●						●	D	$9,379 / $15,302	36%

MISSISSIPPI

GENERAL EDUCATION REQUIREMENTS

INSTITUTION	Comp	Lit	Lang	Gov/Hist	Econ	Math	Sci	GRADE	Tuition & Fees* (In-State/Out-of-State)	Graduation** Rate (4-Year)
Alcorn State University	●					●	●	C	$6,888 / $6,888	15%
Belhaven University	●	●				●	●	B	$24,250	37%
Delta State University	●	●				●	●	B	$6,859 / N/A	19%
Jackson State University	●	●				●	●	B	$7,621 / $18,314	19%
Millsaps College							●	F	$38,930	62%
Mississippi College	●	●				●	●	B	$17,392	43%
Mississippi State University	●	●				●	●	B	$8,318 / $22,358	30%
Mississippi University for Women	●	●				●	●	B	$6,614 / $18,155	25%
Mississippi Valley State University	●	●				●	●	B	$6,422	14%
Rust College	●	●		●			●	B	$9,700	22%
Tougaloo College	●	●				●	●	B	$10,600	27%
University of Mississippi	●	●	●			●	●	B	$8,300 / $23,564	39%
University of Southern Mississippi	●	●				●	●	B	$8,218 / $10,218	26%
William Carey University	●	●						D	$12,300	39%

*   2017–18 tuition and fees. Source: U.S. Department of Education's Integrated Postsecondary Education Data System (IPEDS).
** Four-year graduation rates for first-time, full-time freshmen who enrolled in Fall 2011. Source: College Navigator.

GENERAL EDUCATION REQUIREMENTS

INSTITUTION	Comp	Lit	Lang	Gov/ Hist	Econ	Math	Sci	GRADE	Tuition & Fees* (In-State/Out-of-State)	Graduation** Rate (4-Year)
Drury University						●	●	D	$27,015	40%
Fontbonne University	●			●		●	●	B	$25,460	39%
Lincoln University of Missouri	●			●		●	●	B	$7,632 / $14,172	7%
Lindenwood University	●	●		●		●	●	B	$16,960	32%
Missouri Baptist University	●	●					●	C	$26,020	25%
Missouri Southern State University	●			●		●	●	B	$6,067 / $11,568	13%
Missouri State University	●					●	●	B	$7,306 / $14,746	31%
Missouri University of Science & Technology	●						●	D	$9,246 / $25,918	22%
Missouri Western State University	●			●		●	●	B	$7,570 / $13,465	13%
Northwest Missouri State University	●	●				●	●	B	$7,657 / $12,908	26%
Park University	●					●	●	C	$10,774	7%
Rockhurst University	●	●				●	●	B	$36,590	65%
Saint Louis University	●					●		D	$42,166	68%
Southeast Missouri State University	●					●	●	C	$7,185 / $12,720	29%
Southwest Baptist University	●	●		●	●	●	●	A	$23,358	33%

* 2017–18 tuition and fees. Source: U.S. Department of Education's Integrated Postsecondary Education Data System (IPEDS).
** Four-year graduation rates for first-time, full-time freshmen who enrolled in Fall 2011. Source: College Navigator.

GENERAL EDUCATION REQUIREMENTS

INSTITUTION	Comp	Lit	Lang	Gov/Hist	Econ	Math	Sci	GRADE	Tuition & Fees (In-State/Out-of-State)	Graduation Rate (4-Year)
Truman State University	●	●				●	●	B	$7,656 / $14,440	59%
University of Central Missouri	●	●				●	●	B	$7,520 / $14,150	29%
University of Missouri–Columbia	●						●	D	$9,787 / $26,506	44%
University of Missouri–Kansas City						◐	◐	F	$8,011 / $19,793	23%
University of Missouri–St. Louis	●					◐	◐	D	$9,590 / $25,505	32%
Washington University in St. Louis	●					◐	◐	D	$51,533	88%
Webster University								F	$27,100	48%
Westminster College	●	●				●	●	B	$25,940	57%
William Jewell College	●					●	●	C	$33,620	54%

MONTANA

GENERAL EDUCATION REQUIREMENTS

INSTITUTION	Comp	Lit	Lang	Gov/Hist	Econ	Math	Sci	GRADE	Tuition & Fees* (In-State/Out-of-State)	Graduation** Rate (4-Year)
Carroll College	●	●				●	●	B	$34,480	49%
Montana State University–Billings	●					●	●	C	$5,833 / $18,723	11%
Montana State University–Bozeman						●	●	D	$7,079 / $24,071	24%
Montana State University–Northern	●					●	●	C	$5,861 / $18,171	16%
Rocky Mountain College	●	●				●	●	B	$27,566	40%
University of Montana–Missoula	●					●	●	C	$7,063 / $24,943	29%
University of Montana–Western	●						●	D	$5,502 / $16,716	23%

* *2017–18 tuition and fees. Source: U.S. Department of Education's Integrated Postsecondary Education Data System (IPEDS).*
** *Four-year graduation rates for first-time, full-time freshmen who enrolled in Fall 2011. Source: College Navigator.*

NEBRASKA

GENERAL EDUCATION REQUIREMENTS

INSTITUTION	Comp	Lit	Lang	Gov/ Hist	Econ	Math	Sci	GRADE	Tuition & Fees* (In State/Out of State)	Graduation** Rate (4-Year)
Bellevue University	●			●	●			C	$7,752	17%
Chadron State College							●	F	$7,122 / $7,152	24%
Concordia University–Nebraska	●	●				●	●	B	$31,000	48%
Creighton University	●	●				●	●	B	$38,750	69%
Doane University	●						●	D	$32,250	59%
Hastings College	●						●	D	$29,200	46%
Nebraska Wesleyan University						●	●	D	$32,894	55%
Peru State College	●					●	●	C	$7,260	18%
Union College	●					●	●	C	$23,070	32%
University of Nebraska-Kearney	●					●	●	C	$7,294 / $13,194	28%
University of Nebraska-Lincoln			●				●	D	$8,978 / $24,098	39%
University of Nebraska-Omaha	●						●	D	$7,630 / $20,320	20%
Wayne State College	●					●	●	C	$6,848 / $11,986	28%

*   2017–18 tuition and fees. Source: U.S. Department of Education's Integrated Postsecondary Education Data System (IPEDS).
** Four-year graduation rates for first-time, full-time freshmen who enrolled in Fall 2011. Source: College Navigator.

NEVADA

GENERAL EDUCATION REQUIREMENTS

INSTITUTION	Comp	Lit	Lang	Gov/ Hist	Econ	Math	Sci	GRADE	Tuition & Fees* (In-State/Out-of-State)	Graduation** Rate (4-Year)
Nevada State College	●			●		●	●	B	$5,131 / $16,688	4%
Sierra Nevada College	●					●	●	C	$32,639	5%
University of Nevada–Las Vegas	●			●		●	●	B	$7,665 / $21,853	13%
University of Nevada–Reno	●			●		●	●	B	$7,599 / $21,788	26%

*   2017–18 tuition and fees. Source: U.S. Department of Education's Integrated Postsecondary Education Data System (IPEDS).
** Four-year graduation rates for first-time, full-time freshmen who enrolled in Fall 2011. Source: College Navigator.

NEW HAMPSHIRE

GENERAL EDUCATION REQUIREMENTS

INSTITUTION	Comp	Lit	Lang	Gov/ Hist	Econ	Math	Sci	GRADE	Tuition & Fees* (In-State/Out-of-State)	Graduation** Rate (4-Year)
Dartmouth College	●		●				●	C	$53,368	88%
Franklin Pierce University	●					●	●	C	$34,995	42%
Granite State College	●						●	D	$7,593 / $8,505	23%
Keene State College	●						●	D	$13,868 / $22,614	53%
Plymouth State University	●							F	$13,770 / $22,230	42%
Saint Anselm College	●	●					●	C	$40,200	78%
Southern New Hampshire University	●					●		D	$31,136	42%
Thomas More College of Liberal Arts	●	●	●	●	●	●	●	A	$21,000	61%
University of New Hampshire	●						●	D	$18,067 / $32,637	68%

*   *2017–18 tuition and fees. Source: U.S. Department of Education's Integrated Postsecondary Education Data System (IPEDS).*
** *Four-year graduation rates for first-time, full-time freshmen who enrolled in Fall 2011. Source: College Navigator.*

NEW JERSEY

GENERAL EDUCATION REQUIREMENTS

INSTITUTION	Comp	Lit	Lang	Gov/ Hist	Econ	Math	Sci	GRADE	Tuition & Fees* (In-State/Out-of-State)	Graduation** Rate (4-Year)
Bloomfield College	●					●	●	C	$29,300	13%
Caldwell University	●					●	●	C	$33,950	45%
Drew University	●		●				●	C	$49,468	59%
Fairleigh Dickinson University	●					●	●	C	$39,446	30%
Georgian Court University	●	●					●	C	$32,260	28%
Kean University	●	●					●	C	$12,107 / $19,009	22%
Monmouth University	●	●					●	C	$36,732	57%
Montclair State University	●	●				●		C	$12,455 / $20,567	42%
New Jersey City University	●					●		D	$11,761 / $21,051	13%
Princeton University	●		●				●	C	$47,140	89%
Ramapo College of New Jersey	●	●				●	●	B	$14,080 / $23,214	60%
Rider University	●	●				●	●	B	$41,310	55%
Rowan University	●					●	●	C	$13,422 / $21,890	48%
Rutgers University–Camden	●					●	●	C	$14,501 / $29,924	25%
Rutgers University–New Brunswick	●						●	D	$14,638 / $30,579	60%

* *2017–18 tuition and fees. Source: U.S. Department of Education's Integrated Postsecondary Education Data System (IPEDS).*
** *Four-year graduation rates for first-time, full-time freshmen who enrolled in Fall 2011. Source: College Navigator.*

GENERAL EDUCATION REQUIREMENTS

INSTITUTION	Comp	Lit	Lang	Gov/ Hist	Econ	Math	Sci	GRADE	Tuition & Fees (In-State/Out-of-State)	Graduation Rate (4-Year)
Rutgers University–Newark	●					●	●	C	$14,085 / $30,026	37%
Seton Hall University	●	●				●	●	B	$40,588	56%
Stockton University								F	$13,404 / $20,357	54%
The College of New Jersey							●	F	$16,149 / $27,578	73%
William Paterson University of New Jersey	●	●				●	●	B	$12,652 / $19,654	27%

NEW MEXICO

GENERAL EDUCATION REQUIREMENTS

INSTITUTION	Comp	Lit	Lang	Gov/ Hist	Econ	Math	Sci	GRADE	Tuition & Fees* (In-State/Out-of-State)	Graduation** Rate (4-Year)
Eastern New Mexico University	●						●	D	$6,013 / $11,788	17%
New Mexico Highlands University							●	F	$5,954 / $9,288	8%
New Mexico State University	●					●	●	C	$6,461 / $21,022	18%
St. John's College		●	●	●	●	●	●	A	$52,320	53%
University of New Mexico						●	●	D	$7,448 / $22,038	19%
Western New Mexico University							●	F	$6,066 / $13,539	8%

*   2017–18 tuition and fees. Source: U.S. Department of Education's Integrated Postsecondary Education Data System (IPEDS).
** Four-year graduation rates for first-time, full-time freshmen who enrolled in Fall 2011. Source: College Navigator.

NEW YORK

GENERAL EDUCATION REQUIREMENTS

INSTITUTION	Comp	Lit	Lang	Gov/ Hist	Econ	Math	Sci	GRADE	Tuition & Fees* (In-State/Out-of-State)	Graduation** Rate (4-Year)
Adelphi University	●					●	●	C	$37,170	55%
Alfred University		●					●	D	$28,114	41%
Bard College		●				●	●	C	$52,906	62%
Barnard College	●	●						D	$52,662	87%
Canisius College	●	●						D	$36,454	62%
City University of New York Baruch College	●	●				●	●	B	$7,062 / $14,452	41%
Brooklyn College	●					●	●	C	$7,040 / $14,430	28%
College of Staten Island	●			●		●	●	B	$7,090 / $14,480	20%
Hunter College	●	●	●	●			●	B	$6,982 / $14,372	24%
Lehman College	●							D	$7,010 / $14,400	20%
Medgar Evers College	●	●		●		●	●	B	$6,952 / $14,342	6%
Queens College	●	●					●	C	$7,138 / $14,528	29%
The City College of New York	●					●	●	C	$6,940 / $14,330	12%
York College	●	●				●	●	B	$6,958 / $14,348	7%

* 2017–18 tuition and fees. Source: U.S. Department of Education's Integrated Postsecondary Education Data System (IPEDS).
** Four-year graduation rates for first-time, full-time freshmen who enrolled in Fall 2011. Source: College Navigator.

GENERAL EDUCATION REQUIREMENTS

INSTITUTION	Comp	Lit	Lang	Gov/Hist	Econ	Math	Sci	GRADE	Tuition & Fees (In-State/Out-of-State)	Graduation Rate (4-Year)
Clarkson University						●	●	D	$47,950	56%
Colgate University		●	●			◐	◐	C	$53,980	88%
College of Mount Saint Vincent	●	●				●		C	$37,100	38%
Columbia University	●	●	●	●			●	B	$57,208	88%
Cooper Union	●	●						D	$45,100†	64%
Cornell University	●		●			●	●	B	$52,853	85%
D'Youville College	●			◐	◐	●	●	B	$25,870	26%
Elmira College	●					◐	◐	D	$41,900	55%
Fordham University	●					●	●	C	$50,986	74%
Hamilton College								F	$52,770	90%
Hartwick College							●	F	$44,134	49%
Hobart & William Smith Colleges								F	$53,525	76%
Hofstra University	●						●	D	$43,960	53%
Houghton College		●						F	$31,540	67%
Iona College	●	●						D	$37,682	59%

† *Previously, Cooper Union granted full-tuition scholarships to all admitted students. Starting in Fall 2014, it grants only half-tuition scholarships.*

GENERAL EDUCATION REQUIREMENTS

INSTITUTION	Comp	Lit	Lang	Gov/Hist	Econ	Math	Sci	GRADE	Tuition & Fees (In-State/Out-of-State)	Graduation Rate (4-Year)
Ithaca College	●							F	$42,884	69%
Keuka College	●	●				●		C	$30,946	37%
Le Moyne College	●	●						D	$33,905	64%
Long Island University–Brooklyn	●	●					●	C	$36,978	12%
Long Island University Post	●			◐	◐		●	C	$36,978	28%
Manhattan College	●	●				●	●	B	$41,412	59%
Manhattanville College	●							F	$37,910	49%
Marist College	●					●		D	$36,780	75%
Marymount Manhattan College	●					◐	◐	D	$31,950	39%
Medaille College	●			●		●	●	B	$28,360	37%
Mercy College	●	●				●		C	$18,714	24%
Molloy College	●					●	●	C	$30,310	51%
Nazareth College	●	●					●	C	$33,549	56%
New York University	●	●	●			●	●	B	$50,464	82%
Niagara University	●	●		●			●	B	$31,950	60%
Nyack College	●	●					●	C	$25,350	31%

GENERAL EDUCATION REQUIREMENTS

INSTITUTION	Comp	Lit	Lang	Gov/ Hist	Econ	Math	Sci	GRADE	Tuition & Fees (In-State/Out-of-State)	Graduation Rate (4-Year)
Pace University	●					●	●	C	$43,986	39%
Russell Sage College							●	F	$29,864	45%
Sage College of Albany							●	F	$29,864	45%
Sarah Lawrence College								F	$54,010	74%
Siena College		●				●	●	C	$35,735	74%
Skidmore College	●						●	D	$52,596	84%
St. Bonaventure University	●		●			●	●	B	$33,331	59%
St. Francis College	●							F	$26,188	25%
St. John Fisher College	●							F	$33,120	63%
St. John's University	●	●				●	●	B	$40,520	37%
St. Joseph's College	●					●	●	C	$26,550	62%
St. Lawrence University							●	F	$52,990	82%
State University of New York SUNY–Binghamton University	●					●	●	C	$9,523 / $24,403	73%
SUNY–Buffalo State College	●			●		●		C	$7,976 / $17,626	27%
SUNY–Cortland	●					●	●	C	$8,300 / $17,950	54%

GENERAL EDUCATION REQUIREMENTS

INSTITUTION	Comp	Lit	Lang	Gov/Hist	Econ	Math	Sci	GRADE	Tuition & Fees (In-State/Out-of-State)	Graduation Rate (4-Year)
SUNY–Farmingdale State College	●	●				●		C	$8,076 / $17,726	29%
SUNY–Fredonia	●						●	D	$8,286 / $17,936	48%
SUNY–Geneseo	●	●	●			●	●	B	$8,408 / $18,026	68%
SUNY–New Paltz	●					●	●	C	$7,775 / $17,625	55%
SUNY–Oneonta						●		F	$8,166 / $17,816	60%
SUNY–Oswego	●					●	●	C	$8,191 / $17,841	50%
SUNY–Plattsburgh	●						●	D	$8,148 / $17,798	45%
SUNY–Potsdam	●		●				●	C	$8,221 / $17,871	34%
SUNY–Purchase College	●						●	D	$8,498 / $18,148	56%
SUNY–Stony Brook University	●					●		D	$9,257 / $26,767	53%
SUNY–The College at Brockport							●	F	$8,154 / $17,804	48%
SUNY–The College at Old Westbury	●	●				●		C	$7,883 / $17,533	27%
SUNY–University at Albany	●						●	D	$9,490 / $24,370	56%
SUNY–University at Buffalo						●	●	D	$9,828 / $27,068	57%
Syracuse University	●		●			●	●	B	$46,755	70%
The College of New Rochelle	●					●	●	C	$36,618	23%

GENERAL EDUCATION REQUIREMENTS

INSTITUTION	Comp	Lit	Lang	Gov/ Hist	Econ	Math	Sci	GRADE	Tuition & Fees (In-State/Out-of-State)	Graduation Rate (4-Year)
The College of Saint Rose	•						•	D	$31,612	46%
The King's College	•			•	•	•	•	B	$35,400	45%
Touro College		•	•			•	•	B	$18,200	44%
Union College	•						•	D	$53,490	79%
United States Merchant Marine Academy	•	•		•	•	•	•	A	$1,020	74%
United States Military Academy	•	•		•	•	•	•	A	$0	82%
University of Rochester	•							F	$52,020	76%
Utica College	•	•				•	•	B	$20,676	35%
Vassar College								F	$55,210	85%
Wagner College		•					•	D	$45,380	63%
Wells College	•						•	D	$39,600	46%
Yeshiva University	•	•	•				•	B	$42,000	76%
Yeshiva University–Stern College for Women	•		•			•	•	B	$42,000	76%

GENERAL EDUCATION REQUIREMENTS

INSTITUTION	Comp	Lit	Lang	Gov/Hist	Econ	Math	Sci	GRADE	Tuition & Fees* (In-State/Out-of-State)	Graduation** Rate (4-Year)
Appalachian State University		•					•	D	$7,302 / $22,109	51%
Barton College	•	•				•	•	B	$29,998	40%
Belmont Abbey College	•	•		•		•	•	B	$18,500	34%
Bennett College	•	•				•	•	B	$18,513	22%
Brevard College	•	•				•	•	B	$28,640	23%
Campbell University	•	•	•			•	•	B	$31,190	37%
Catawba College	•		•			•	•	B	$29,920	35%
Chowan University	•	•		•			•	B	$24,480	11%
Davidson College	•		•			•	•	B	$49,949	88%
Duke University	•		•			•	•	B	$53,500	88%
East Carolina University	•					•	•	C	$7,143 / $23,420	37%
Elizabeth City State University	•	•				•	•	B	$4,986 / $18,130	23%
Elon University	•	•				•	•	B	$34,273	78%
Fayetteville State University	•					•	•	C	$5,183 / $16,791	17%
Gardner-Webb University	•	•	•	◑	◑	•	•	A	$30,700	4%

* *2017–18 tuition and fees. Source: U.S. Department of Education's Integrated Postsecondary Education Data System (IPEDS).*
** *Four-year graduation rates for first-time, full-time freshmen who enrolled in Fall 2011. Source: College Navigator.*

GENERAL EDUCATION REQUIREMENTS

INSTITUTION	Comp	Lit	Lang	Gov/ Hist	Econ	Math	Sci	GRADE	Tuition & Fees (In-State/Out-of-State)	Graduation Rate (4-Year)
Greensboro College	●					●	●	C	$29,120	16%
Guilford College	●						●	D	$35,563	45%
High Point University	●	●				●	●	B	$34,005	59%
Johnson C. Smith University	●					●	●	C	$18,236	32%
Lees-McRae College	●	●				●	●	B	$25,878	29%
Lenoir-Rhyne University	●					●	●	C	$35,350	32%
Mars Hill University	●	○		○		●	●	B	$31,804	22%
Meredith College	●	●	●			●	●	B	$35,916	53%
Methodist University	●	●				●	●	B	$32,860	17%
Mid-Atlantic Christian University	●					○	○	D	$14,080	17%
Montreat College	●	●				●	●	B	$25,730	26%
North Carolina Agricultural & Technical State U.	●					●	●	C	$6,526 / $19,416	17%
North Carolina Central University	●					●	●	C	$6,399 / $19,106	20%
North Carolina State University						●		F	$9,058 / $27,406	50%
North Carolina Wesleyan College	●	●				●	●	B	$29,900	23%

GENERAL EDUCATION REQUIREMENTS

INSTITUTION	Comp	Lit	Lang	Gov/Hist	Econ	Math	Sci	GRADE	Tuition & Fees (In-State/Out-of-State)	Graduation Rate (4-Year)
Pfeiffer University	●	●					●	C	$29,574	35%
Queens University of Charlotte	●							F	$33,532	46%
Saint Augustine's University	●			◐	◐	●	●	B	$17,890	22%
Salem College	●		●			●	●	B	$28,566	56%
Shaw University	●					●	●	C	$16,480	8%
St. Andrews University	●					●	●	C	$25,874	27%
University of Mount Olive	●	●				●	●	B	$19,700	34%
University of North Carolina–Asheville	●	●				●	●	B	$7,145 / $23,868	42%
University of North Carolina–Chapel Hill	●		●			●	●	B	$9,005 / $34,588	84%
University of North Carolina–Charlotte	●					●	●	C	$6,832 / $20,266	29%
University of North Carolina–Greensboro	●	●	●			●	●	B	$7,250 / $22,409	30%
University of North Carolina–Pembroke	●					●	●	C	$6,014 / $17,605	20%
University of North Carolina–Wilmington	●						●	D	$7,000 / $21,065	54%
Wake Forest University	●		●			◐	◐	C	$51,400	84%
Warren Wilson College						●	●	D	$35,244	40%

GENERAL EDUCATION REQUIREMENTS

INSTITUTION	Comp	Lit	Lang	Gov/ Hist	Econ	Math	Sci	GRADE	Tuition & Fees (In-State/Out-of-State)	Graduation Rate (4-Year)
Western Carolina University	●						●	D	$6,897 / $17,290	40%
William Peace University	●					●	●	C	$28,700	32%
Wingate University	●	●			●	●	●	B	$31,120	41%
Winston-Salem State University						●	●	D	$5,941 / $16,188	21%

NORTH DAKOTA

GENERAL EDUCATION REQUIREMENTS

INSTITUTION	Comp	Lit	Lang	Gov/ Hist	Econ	Math	Sci	GRADE	Tuition & Fees* (In-State/Out-of-State)	Graduation** Rate (4-Year)
Dickinson State University	●	●				●	●	B	$6,554 / $9,226	12%
Mayville State University						●		F	$6,456 / $9,084	15%
Minot State University	●					●	●	C	$6,810	17%
North Dakota State University	●					●	●	C	$8,666 / $20,692	32%
University of Mary	●			●		●	●	B	$18,224	39%
University of North Dakota	●						●	D	$8,447 / $20,047	26%
Valley City State University	●					●	●	C	$7,406 / $16,579	21%

*   2017–18 tuition and fees. Source: U.S. Department of Education's Integrated Postsecondary Education Data System (IPEDS).
** Four-year graduation rates for first-time, full-time freshmen who enrolled in Fall 2011. Source: College Navigator.

GENERAL EDUCATION REQUIREMENTS

INSTITUTION	Comp	Lit	Lang	Gov/ Hist	Econ	Math	Sci	GRADE	Tuition & Fees* (In-State/Out-of-State)	Graduation** Rate (4-Year)
Ashland University	●						●	D	$20,700	48%
Baldwin Wallace University	●					●	●	C	$31,668	50%
Bluffton University	●	●					●	C	$31,672	45%
Bowling Green State University	●					●	●	C	$11,057 / $18,593	35%
Capital University							●	F	$34,600	50%
Case Western Reserve University						●		F	$47,500	66%
Cedarville University	●	●		●		●	●	B	$29,156	60%
Central State University	●			●		●	●	B	$6,246 / $8,096	10%
Cleveland State University	●						●	D	$9,778 / $13,829	22%
College of Wooster						◐	◐	F	$48,600	72%
Defiance College	●					●	●	C	$32,190	33%
Denison University	●						●	D	$50,440	83%
Franciscan University of Steubenville		●		●	◐	◐	●	B	$26,430	68%
Hiram College							●	F	$34,300	50%
John Carroll University	●							F	$39,990	72%

* 2017–18 tuition and fees. Source: U.S. Department of Education's Integrated Postsecondary Education Data System (IPEDS).
** Four-year graduation rates for first-time, full-time freshmen who enrolled in Fall 2011. Source: College Navigator.

GENERAL EDUCATION REQUIREMENTS

INSTITUTION	Comp	Lit	Lang	Gov/ Hist	Econ	Math	Sci	GRADE	Tuition & Fees (In-State/Out-of-State)	Graduation Rate (4-Year)
Kent State University	●					●	●	C	$10,012 / $18,544	34%
Kenyon College						⊖	⊖	F	$53,560	86%
Miami University	●		●				●	C	$14,958 / $34,211	67%
Muskingum University							●	F	$27,646	34%
Oberlin College						⊖	⊖	F	$53,460	75%
Ohio Dominican University	●					●	●	C	$31,080	38%
Ohio Northern University	●					●	●	C	$30,990	55%
Ohio University	●						●	D	$11,896 / $21,360	44%
Ohio Wesleyan University	●						●	D	$44,690	62%
Otterbein University	●	●					●	C	$31,874	53%
Shawnee State University	●	●					●	C	$7,439 / $13,247	13%
The Ohio State University	●		●			●	●	B	$10,592 / $29,696	59%
Tiffin University		●				●		D	$24,000	22%
University of Akron	●					●	●	C	$10,270 / $18,801	17%
University of Cincinnati	●		●				●	C	$11,000 / $27,334	33%
University of Dayton	●					●	●	C	$41,750	60%

GENERAL EDUCATION REQUIREMENTS

INSTITUTION	Comp	Lit	Lang	Gov/Hist	Econ	Math	Sci	GRADE	Tuition & Fees (In-State/Out-of-State)	Graduation Rate (4-Year)
University of Findlay	●					●		D	$33,320	49%
University of Rio Grande	●					●	●	C	$26,175	17%
University of Toledo	●	●				●	●	B	$9,547 / $18,885	22%
Walsh University	●						●	D	$29,150	45%
Wilberforce University	●	●					●	C	$13,250	7%
Wittenberg University	●						●	D	$38,730	61%
Wright State University	●					●	●	C	$8,730 / $17,098	19%
Xavier University	●	●				●	●	B	$37,230	61%
Youngstown State University	●					●	●	C	$8,451 / $8,811	14%

OKLAHOMA

GENERAL EDUCATION REQUIREMENTS

INSTITUTION	Comp	Lit	Lang	Gov/Hist	Econ	Math	Sci	GRADE	Tuition & Fees* (In-State/Out-of-State)	Graduation** Rate (4-Year)
Cameron University	●			●	●	●	●	B	$6,180 / $15,510	9%
East Central University	●			●		●	●	B	$6,600 / $15,720	20%
Langston University	●	●		●		●	●	B	$5,936 / $13,286	8%
Northeastern State University	●			●		●	●	B	$6,327 / $14,022	13%
Northwestern Oklahoma State University	●			●		●	●	B	$7,066 / $14,183	14%
Oklahoma City University	●	●		●		●	●	B	$30,726	50%
Oklahoma Panhandle State University	●			●	●	●	●	B	$6,196 / N/A	15%
Oklahoma State University	●					●	●	B	$8,738 / $23,776	38%
Oklahoma Wesleyan University	●	●		●		●	●	B	$26,090	2%
Oral Roberts University	●					●	●	C	$26,792	47%
Rogers State University	●			●		●	●	B	$6,870 / $15,210	11%
Southeastern Oklahoma State University	●			●		●	●	B	$6,750 / $15,390	10%
Southwestern Oklahoma State University	●			●		●	●	B	$7,005 / $13,905	16%
University of Central Oklahoma	●			●		●	●	B	$7,100 / $17,447	14%
University of Oklahoma	●		●	●		●	●	B	$11,538 / $26,919	41%

* 2017–18 tuition and fees. Source: U.S. Department of Education's Integrated Postsecondary Education Data System (IPEDS).
** Four-year graduation rates for first-time, full-time freshmen who enrolled in Fall 2011. Source: College Navigator.

GENERAL EDUCATION REQUIREMENTS

INSTITUTION	Comp	Lit	Lang	Gov/Hist	Econ	Math	Sci	GRADE	Tuition & Fees (In-State/Out-of-State)	Graduation Rate (4-Year)
University of Science and Arts of Oklahoma	●	●		●	●	●	●	A	$7,200 / $17,550	21%
University of Tulsa	●						●	D	$41,509	50%

GENERAL EDUCATION REQUIREMENTS

INSTITUTION	Comp	Lit	Lang	Gov/Hist	Econ	Math	Sci	GRADE	Tuition & Fees* (In-State/Out-of-State)	Graduation** Rate (4-Year)
Concordia University	●					●	●	C	$30,270	37%
Corban University	●	●		●			●	B	$31,640	41%
Eastern Oregon University	●						●	D	$8,362 / $19,682	20%
George Fox University		●					●	D	$35,016	63%
Lewis & Clark College		●	●				●	C	$46,988	75%
Linfield College							●	F	$41,682	65%
Oregon State University	●						●	D	$10,967 / $29,457	33%
Pacific University	●						●	D	$42,594	55%
Portland State University								F	$8,783 / $26,130	21%
Reed College		●					●	D	$54,200	65%
Southern Oregon University	●					●	●	C	$9,287 / $24,630	23%
University of Oregon	●		◐			◐		D	$11,931 / $34,611	52%
University of Portland	●	●					●	C	$44,026	74%
Warner Pacific College	●						●	D	$24,500	28%

* 2017–18 tuition and fees. Source: U.S. Department of Education's Integrated Postsecondary Education Data System (IPEDS).
** Four-year graduation rates for first-time, full-time freshmen who enrolled in Fall 2011. Source: College Navigator.

GENERAL EDUCATION REQUIREMENTS

INSTITUTION	Comp	Lit	Lang	Gov/ Hist	Econ	Math	Sci	GRADE	Tuition & Fees* (In-State/Out-of-State)	Graduation** Rate (4-Year)
Western Oregon University		•					•	D	$9,198 / $25,653	22%
Willamette University			•			•	•	C	$48,158	66%

PENNSYLVANIA

GENERAL EDUCATION REQUIREMENTS

INSTITUTION	Comp	Lit	Lang	Gov/ Hist	Econ	Math	Sci	GRADE	Tuition & Fees* (In-State/Out-of-State)	Graduation** Rate (4-Year)
Albright College	●		●				●	C	$43,454	44%
Allegheny College	●							F	$45,970	69%
Alvernia University	●					●	●	C	$33,640	44%
Arcadia University	●					●	●	C	$42,330	63%
Bloomsburg University of Pennsylvania	●					●	●	C	$10,500 / $21,980	37%
Bryn Athyn College of the New Church	●	●					●	C	$21,126	38%
Bryn Mawr College						◐	◐	F	$50,500	76%
Bucknell University	●						●	D	$53,986	86%
Cabrini University						●	●	D	$31,350	47%
California University of Pennsylvania	●							F	$10,840 / $15,326	39%
Carnegie Mellon University	●					●	●	C	$53,910	76%
Cedar Crest College	●					●	●	C	$38,092	38%
Chestnut Hill College	●						●	D	$35,180	47%
Cheyney University of Pennsylvania	●						●	D	$12,104 / $18,386	8%
Clarion University of Pennsylvania	●						●	D	$10,890 / $15,636	33%

* 2017–18 tuition and fees. Source: U.S. Department of Education's Integrated Postsecondary Education Data System (IPEDS).
** Four-year graduation rates for first-time, full-time freshmen who enrolled in Fall 2011. Source: College Navigator.

GENERAL EDUCATION REQUIREMENTS

INSTITUTION	Comp	Lit	Lang	Gov/Hist	Econ	Math	Sci	GRADE	Tuition & Fees (In-State/Out-of-State)	Graduation Rate (4-Year)
Delaware Valley University	●	●			●	●	●	B	$38,000	46%
DeSales University	●	●					●	C	$35,900	62%
Dickinson College			●			◐	◐	D	$52,955	80%
Drexel University	●					●	●	C	$52,002	27%
Duquesne University	●	●					●	C	$36,394	68%
East Stroudsburg University of Pennsylvania	●						●	D	$10,098 / $21,778	32%
Eastern University	●						●	D	$32,145	57%
Edinboro University of Pennsylvania	●						●	D	$10,282 / $14,668	27%
Elizabethtown College	●					●	●	C	$45,350	69%
Franklin & Marshall College			●				●	D	$54,380	80%
Gannon University	●	●				●	●	B	$30,932	53%
Gettysburg College							●	F	$52,640	79%
Grove City College	●	●				●	●	B	$17,254	78%
Haverford College	●					◐	◐	D	$52,994	87%
Holy Family University	●	●				●	●	B	$30,346	44%
Immaculata University	●						●	D	$27,350	47%

GENERAL EDUCATION REQUIREMENTS

INSTITUTION	Comp	Lit	Lang	Gov/ Hist	Econ	Math	Sci	GRADE	Tuition & Fees (In-State/Out-of-State)	Graduation Rate (4-Year)
Indiana University of Pennsylvania	●	●				●	●	B	$12,119 / $17,271	39%
Juniata College	●					◐	◐	D	$43,875	80%
King's College	●	●					●	C	$35,830	62%
Kutztown University of Pennsylvania	●						●	D	$9,987 / $13,975	35%
La Salle University	●	●		◐	◐	●	●	B	$29,500	62%
Lafayette College	●							F	$51,600	86%
Lebanon Valley College	●							F	$42,180	69%
Lehigh University						●	●	D	$50,740	76%
Lincoln University of Pennsylvania	●	●		●			●	B	$11,379 / $17,151	30%
Lock Haven University of Pennsylvania	●						●	D	$10,576 / $20,056	35%
Lycoming College	●					●	●	C	$38,618	59%
Mansfield University of Pennsylvania	●					●	●	C	$12,316 / $22,008	39%
Marywood University	●	●				●	●	B	$33,940	55%
Mercyhurst University	●							F	$36,320	62%
Messiah College		●					●	D	$34,160	76%
Millersville University of Pennsylvania						●	●	D	$11,858 / $21,560	36%

GENERAL EDUCATION REQUIREMENTS

INSTITUTION	Comp	Lit	Lang	Gov/ Hist	Econ	Math	Sci	GRADE	Tuition & Fees (In-State/Out-of-State)	Graduation Rate (4-Year)
Misericordia University	●	●				●	●	B	$31,660	71%
Moravian College						●		F	$42,024	59%
Muhlenberg College	●					◐	◐	D	$50,830	84%
Neumann University	●	●				●	●	B	$30,050	38%
Pennsylvania State University	●					●	●	C	$18,436 / $33,664	67%
Point Park University	●	●				●	●	B	$30,130	49%
Robert Morris University		●			●	●		C	$29,420	47%
Rosemont College	●						●	D	$19,486	51%
Saint Francis University	●	●					●	C	$35,066	59%
Saint Joseph's University	●	●						D	$43,880	76%
Saint Vincent College	●		●			●	●	B	$34,430	62%
Shippensburg University of Pennsylvania	●						●	D	$12,086 / $20,186	34%
Slippery Rock University of Pennsylvania	●	●					●	C	$10,205 / $14,193	50%
Susquehanna University	●	●				●	●	B	$45,470	65%
Swarthmore College	●					◐	◐	D	$50,822	89%
Temple University		●						F	$16,658 / $28,418	45%

GENERAL EDUCATION REQUIREMENTS

INSTITUTION	Comp	Lit	Lang	Gov/ Hist	Econ	Math	Sci	GRADE	Tuition & Fees (In-State/Out-of-State)	Graduation Rate (4-Year)
Thiel College	●	●					●	C	$30,830	43%
University of Pennsylvania	●		●				●	C	$53,534	86%
University of Pittsburgh–Bradford	●	●					●	C	$13,900 / $25,144	33%
University of Pittsburgh–Greensburg	●	●	●				●	B	$13,870 / $25,114	19%
University of Pittsburgh–Johnstown	●							F	$13,876 / $25,120	32%
University of Pittsburgh–Pittsburgh	●						●	D	$19,080 / $30,642	65%
University of Scranton	●							F	$43,310	72%
Ursinus College		●				◐	◐	D	$50,360	75%
Villanova University	●	●				●	●	B	$51,284	87%
Washington & Jefferson College	●	●					●	C	$46,628	67%
West Chester University of Pennsylvania	●					●	●	C	$10,111 / $21,591	48%
Westminster College	●		●			●	●	B	$36,276	60%
Widener University	●						●	D	$44,166	44%
Wilkes University	●	●				●	●	B	$34,896	47%
Wilson College	●					●	●	C	$24,452	47%
York College of Pennsylvania							●	F	$19,430	37%

RHODE ISLAND

GENERAL EDUCATION REQUIREMENTS

INSTITUTION	Comp	Lit	Lang	Gov/ Hist	Econ	Math	Sci	GRADE	Tuition & Fees* (In-State/Out-of-State)	Graduation** Rate (4-Year)
Brown University								F	$53,419	86%
Bryant University	•	•			•	•	•	B	$42,109	73%
Providence College		•				•	•	C	$48,764	80%
Rhode Island College	•	•				•	•	B	$8,776 / $21,289	20%
Roger Williams University	•	•					•	C	$33,336	55%
University of Rhode Island								F	$13,792 / $30,042	47%

*   2017–18 tuition and fees. Source: U.S. Department of Education's Integrated Postsecondary Education Data System (IPEDS).
** Four-year graduation rates for first-time, full-time freshmen who enrolled in Fall 2011. Source: College Navigator.

SOUTH CAROLINA

GENERAL EDUCATION REQUIREMENTS

INSTITUTION	Comp	Lit	Lang	Gov/Hist	Econ	Math	Sci	GRADE	Tuition & Fees* (In-State/Out-of-State)	Graduation** Rate (4-Year)
Allen University	●	●				●	●	B	$13,140	13%
Anderson University	●					●	●	C	$26,970	52%
Charleston Southern University	●	●				●	●	B	$24,840	24%
Claflin University	●	●				●	●	B	$16,480	39%
Clemson University	●	●				●	●	B	$15,116 / $36,058	59%
Coastal Carolina University	●			●		●	●	B	$11,200 / $25,872	26%
Coker College	●						●	D	$28,684	40%
College of Charleston	●		●			●	●	B	$12,422 / $30,810	56%
Converse College		●	●				●	C	$17,680	67%
Erskine College	●	●				●	●	B	$34,560	56%
Francis Marion University	●					●	●	C	$10,742 / $20,918	14%
Furman University	●					●	●	C	$48,348	73%
Lander University	●	●				●	●	B	$11,700 / $21,300	24%
Limestone College	●	●				●	●	B	$25,025	12%
Newberry College	◐	◐				●	●	C	$25,900	28%

*   2017–18 tuition and fees. Source: U.S. Department of Education's Integrated Postsecondary Education Data System (IPEDS).
** Four-year graduation rates for first-time, full-time freshmen who enrolled in Fall 2011. Source: College Navigator.

GENERAL EDUCATION REQUIREMENTS

INSTITUTION	Comp	Lit	Lang	Gov/Hist	Econ	Math	Sci	GRADE	Tuition & Fees (In-State/Out-of-State)	Graduation Rate (4-Year)
North Greenville University	●	●					●	C	$19,150	38%
Presbyterian College	●	●	●				●	B	$37,842	62%
South Carolina State University	●	●		◒	◒	●	●	B	$10,740 / $21,120	15%
The Citadel	●	●	●			●	●	B	$12,056 / $33,819	64%
University of South Carolina–Aiken	●	●		●		●	●	B	$10,502 / $20,702	21%
University of South Carolina–Beaufort	●	●				●	●	B	$10,647 / $21,423	13%
University of South Carolina–Columbia	●					●	●	C	$11,862 / $31,962	58%
University of South Carolina–Upstate	●					●	●	C	$11,520 / $22,848	25%
Winthrop University	●					●	●	C	$15,220 / $29,136	38%
Wofford College	●	●					●	C	$41,955	77%

SOUTH DAKOTA

GENERAL EDUCATION REQUIREMENTS

INSTITUTION	Comp	Lit	Lang	Gov/ Hist	Econ	Math	Sci	GRADE	Tuition & Fees* (In-State/Out-of-State)	Graduation** Rate (4-Year)
Augustana University		•					•	D	$31,960	55%
Black Hills State University	•					•	•	C	$8,602 / $11,602	13%
Dakota State University	•					•	•	C	$9,147 / $12,077	18%
Mount Marty College	•						•	D	$26,310	47%
Northern State University	•					•	•	C	$8,280 / $11,210	26%
South Dakota State University	•					•	•	C	$8,441 / $11,689	31%
University of Sioux Falls	•	•				•	•	B	$27,980	38%
University of South Dakota	•					•	•	C	$8,772 / $12,019	39%

*   2017–18 tuition and fees. Source: U.S. Department of Education's Integrated Postsecondary Education Data System (IPEDS).
** Four-year graduation rates for first-time, full-time freshmen who enrolled in Fall 2011. Source: College Navigator.

TENNESSEE

GENERAL EDUCATION REQUIREMENTS

INSTITUTION	Comp	Lit	Lang	Gov/ Hist	Econ	Math	Sci	GRADE	Tuition & Fees* (In-State/Out-of-State)	Graduation** Rate (4-Year)
Austin Peay State University	●	●				●	●	B	$7,913 / $23,153	18%
Belmont University	●					●	●	C	$32,820	58%
Bethel University	●	●					●	C	$16,552	24%
Bryan College	●					●	●	C	$25,600	43%
Carson-Newman University	●	●					●	C	$27,400	37%
Christian Brothers University	●	●				●	●	B	$31,870	25%
Cumberland University	●						●	D	$21,810	37%
East Tennessee State University	●	●		●		●	●	B	$8,679 / $26,463	21%
Fisk University	●		●			●	●	B	$21,480	42%
King University	●		●				●	C	$28,572	38%
Lane College	●	●				●	●	B	$10,690	10%
Lee University	●	●		●			●	B	$16,730	37%
LeMoyne-Owen College	●	●		●		●	●	B	$11,196	7%
Lincoln Memorial University	●	●					●	C	$21,410	42%
Lipscomb University	●	●					●	C	$30,932	46%

* 2017–18 tuition and fees. Source: U.S. Department of Education's Integrated Postsecondary Education Data System (IPEDS).
** Four-year graduation rates for first-time, full-time freshmen who enrolled in Fall 2011. Source: College Navigator.

GENERAL EDUCATION REQUIREMENTS

INSTITUTION	Comp	Lit	Lang	Gov/ Hist	Econ	Math	Sci	GRADE	Tuition & Fees (In-State/Out-of-State)	Graduation Rate (4-Year)
Maryville College	●	●				●	●	B	$34,196	48%
Middle Tennessee State University		●		●		●	●	B	$8,612 / $26,348	20%
Rhodes College	●	●	●			●	●	B	$46,504	79%
Sewanee: The University of the South	●	●	●			●		B	$45,120	72%
Southern Adventist University	●					●	●	C	$21,550	20%
Tennessee State University	●	●		●		●	●	B	$7,776 / $21,132	13%
Tennessee Technological University		●		●		●	●	B	$8,513 / $24,377	25%
Tusculum University	●					●	●	C	$23,700	18%
Union University	●	●					●	C	$31,510	62%
University of Memphis	●	●					●	C	$9,317 / $21,029	19%
University of Tennessee-Chattanooga	●					●	●	C	$8,664 / $24,782	22%
University of Tennessee-Knoxville	●		●			●		C	$12,970 / $31,390	46%
University of Tennessee-Martin	●						●	D	$9,236 / $14,996	23%
Vanderbilt University	●						●	D	$47,664	86%

TEXAS

GENERAL EDUCATION REQUIREMENTS

INSTITUTION	Comp	Lit	Lang	Gov/ Hist	Econ	Math	Sci	GRADE	Tuition & Fees* (In-State/Out-of-State)	Graduation** Rate (4-Year)
Abilene Christian University	●	●				●		C	$33,330	48%
Angelo State University				●			●	D	$7,201 / $17,161	25%
Austin College			●				●	D	$38,800	62%
Baylor University	●	●	●	●		●	●	A	$43,790	60%
Concordia University Texas	●	●		●		●	●	B	$30,600	26%
Dallas Baptist University	●	●		●			●	B	$27,480	44%
East Texas Baptist University	●	●		●		●	●	B	$25,470	19%
Hardin-Simmons University	●	●		●		●	●	B	$27,440	35%
Houston Baptist University	●	●		●		●	●	B	$31,730	29%
Lamar University	●			●		●	●	B	$8,314 / $18,274	10%
LeTourneau University	●					●	●	C	$29,320	49%
Midwestern State University				●		●	●	C	$8,694 / $10,644	20%
Prairie View A&M University	●			●		●	●	B	$9,959 / $23,488	13%
Rice University								F	$45,608	83%
Sam Houston State University				●		●	●	C	$8,062 / $18,022	29%

*   *2017–18 tuition and fees. Source: U.S. Department of Education's Integrated Postsecondary Education Data System (IPEDS).*
** *Four-year graduation rates for first-time, full-time freshmen who enrolled in Fall 2011. Source: College Navigator.*

GENERAL EDUCATION REQUIREMENTS

INSTITUTION	Comp	Lit	Lang	Gov/ Hist	Econ	Math	Sci	GRADE	Tuition & Fees (In-State/Out-of-State)	Graduation Rate (4-Year)
Southern Methodist University	●					●	●	C	$52,498	71%
Southwestern University			●			◐	◐	D	$40,560	67%
St. Edward's University	●						●	D	$43,300	52%
St. Mary's University	●	●				●	●	B	$29,300	47%
Stephen F. Austin State University	●			●		●	●	B	$7,716 / $17,676	26%
Sul Ross State University	●			●			●	C	$8,072 / $20,522	13%
Tarleton State University	●			●		●	●	B	$7,367 / $17,111	26%
Texas A&M International University	●			●		●	●	B	$7,143 / $17,411	22%
Texas A&M University–College Station				●		●	●	C	$11,234 / $36,606	54%
Texas A&M University–Commerce	●						●	C	$8,434 / $20,884	24%
Texas A&M University–Corpus Christi	●			●		●	●	B	$8,750 / $18,925	18%
Texas A&M University–Kingsville				●			●	D	$8,462 / $22,102	19%
Texas Christian University	●					●	●	C	$44,760	69%
Texas Southern University	●	●		●		●	●	B	$9,173 / $21,623	8%
Texas State University	●	●		●		●	●	B	$9,985 / $21,605	27%
Texas Tech University	●		●	●		●	●	B	$8,860 / $18,652	35%

GENERAL EDUCATION REQUIREMENTS

INSTITUTION	Comp	Lit	Lang	Gov/ Hist	Econ	Math	Sci	GRADE	Tuition & Fees (In-State/Out-of-State)	Graduation Rate (4-Year)
Texas Woman's University	●			●		●	●	B	$7,486 / $17,446	19%
Trinity University			●				●	D	$41,344	72%
University of Dallas	●	●	●	●	●	●	●	A	$38,716	65%
University of Houston-Downtown	●			●			●	C	$6,470 / $16,430	3%
University of Houston-Houston	●			●		●	●	B	$9,706 / $22,066	25%
University of Houston-Victoria	●			●			●	B	$6,805 / $17,750	7%
University of Mary Hardin-Baylor		●					●	D	$27,600	32%
University of North Texas	●			●		●	●	B	$10,544 / $20,504	29%
University of St. Thomas	●	●		●		●	●	B	$32,660	31%
University of Texas-Arlington	●			●		●	●	B	$9,952 / $25,152	22%
University of Texas-Austin		●		●		●	●	B	$10,398 / $36,744	58%
University of Texas-Dallas				●		●	●	C	$11,528 / $29,656	52%
University of Texas-El Paso	●			●		●	●	B	$7,851 / $21,596	14%
University of Texas-Permian Basin	●			●		●	●	B	$5,782 / $6,622	24%
University of Texas-San Antonio	●			●		●	●	B	$7,969 / $19,168	15%
University of Texas-Tyler				●		●	●	C	$7,822 / $20,872	25%

GENERAL EDUCATION REQUIREMENTS

INSTITUTION	Comp	Lit	Lang	Gov/Hist	Econ	Math	Sci	GRADE	Tuition & Fees (In-State/Out-of-State)	Graduation Rate (4-Year)
University of the Incarnate Word	●	●				●	●	B	$29,990	29%
Wayland Baptist University	●			●			●	C	$18,510	6%
West Texas A&M University				●			●	D	$7,846 / $9,117	25%

UTAH

GENERAL EDUCATION REQUIREMENTS

INSTITUTION	Comp	Lit	Lang	Gov/ Hist	Econ	Math	Sci	GRADE	Tuition & Fees* (In-State/Out-of-State)	Graduation** Rate (4-Year)
Brigham Young University	●			●			●	C	$5,460	23%
Dixie State University	●			●			●	C	$5,080 / $14,548	11%
Southern Utah University	●			●		●	●	B	$6,676 / $20,288	19%
University of Utah	●			●		●		C	$8,884 / $28,127	31%
Utah State University	●			◒	◒		●	C	$7,870 / $21,520	18%
Utah Valley University	●			●			●	C	$5,652 / $16,066	10%
Weber State University	●			●			●	C	$5,712 / $15,260	12%
Westminster College								F	$33,860	51%

*   2017–18 tuition and fees. Source: U.S. Department of Education's Integrated Postsecondary Education Data System (IPEDS).
** Four-year graduation rates for first-time, full-time freshmen who enrolled in Fall 2011. Source: College Navigator.

VERMONT

GENERAL EDUCATION REQUIREMENTS

INSTITUTION	Comp	Lit	Lang	Gov/ Hist	Econ	Math	Sci	GRADE	Tuition & Fees* (In-State/Out-of-State)	Graduation** Rate (4-Year)
Bennington College								F	$51,920	56%
Castleton University	•	•						D	$11,970 / $27,522	38%
Champlain College	•							F	$39,818	50%
Johnson State College	•						•	D	$11,730 / $24,690	27%
Lyndon State College	•						•	D	$11,730 / $23,898	26%
Middlebury College								F	$52,496	86%
Norwich University	•	•				•	•	B	$38,662	51%
Saint Michael's College	•							F	$43,640	71%
University of Vermont						•	•	D	$17,740 / $41,356	62%

*   2017–18 tuition and fees. Source: U.S. Department of Education's Integrated Postsecondary Education Data System (IPEDS).
** Four-year graduation rates for first-time, full-time freshmen who enrolled in Fall 2011. Source: College Navigator.

GENERAL EDUCATION REQUIREMENTS

INSTITUTION	Comp	Lit	Lang	Gov/Hist	Econ	Math	Sci	GRADE	Tuition & Fees* (In-State/Out-of-State)	Graduation** Rate (4-Year)
Averett University	•	•				•	•	B	$33,350	34%
Bluefield College	•	•		•	•	•	•	A	$24,800	15%
Bridgewater College		•					•	D	$33,820	53%
Christendom College		•	•			•	•	B	$25,460†	73%†
Christopher Newport University	•	•	•	•	•	•	•	A	$13,654 / $25,850	63%
College of William & Mary	•		•			•		C	$22,044 / $43,670	85%
Eastern Mennonite University	•							F	$35,800	54%
Emory & Henry College								F	$33,700	37%
Ferrum College	•	•				•	•	B	$33,025	26%
George Mason University	•	•				•	•	B	$11,924 / $34,370	49%
Hampden-Sydney College	•	•	•			•	•	B	$43,940	60%
Hampton University	•	•				•	•	B	$25,441	38%
Hollins University	•							F	$38,285	58%
James Madison University	•	•		•		•	•	B	$10,830 / $27,230	58%

* *2017–18 tuition and fees. Source: U.S. Department of Education's Integrated Postsecondary Education Data System (IPEDS).*
** *Four-year graduation rates for first-time, full-time freshmen who enrolled in Fall 2011. Source: College Navigator.*
† *Data are reported from information provided by Christendom College staff.*

GENERAL EDUCATION REQUIREMENTS

INSTITUTION	Comp	Lit	Lang	Gov/ Hist	Econ	Math	Sci	GRADE	Tuition & Fees (In-State/Out-of-State)	Graduation Rate (4-Year)
Liberty University	●						●	D	$21,310	32%
Longwood University	●	●	●				●	B	$12,720 / $27,660	48%
Mary Baldwin University	●						●	D	$31,110	41%
Marymount University	●						●	D	$30,876	40%
Norfolk State University	●						●	D	$9,036 / $20,478	15%
Old Dominion University	●	●				●	●	B	$10,050 / $27,900	27%
Radford University	●						●	D	$10,627 / $22,709	38%
Randolph College							●	F	$38,155	54%
Randolph-Macon College	●		●			●	●	B	$40,000	60%
Regent University	●	●		●	●	●	●	A	$17,288	44%
Roanoke College			●			●		C	$42,819	63%
Shenandoah University	●		●			●	●	B	$31,920	47%
Sweet Briar College	●	●	●				●	B	$37,155	53%
University of Lynchburg	●	●				●		B	$37,690	51%
University of Mary Washington			●				●	D	$12,128 / $27,374	60%
University of Richmond			●			●	●	C	$50,910	83%

GENERAL EDUCATION REQUIREMENTS

INSTITUTION	Comp	Lit	Lang	Gov/Hist	Econ	Math	Sci	GRADE	Tuition & Fees (In-State/Out-of-State)	Graduation Rate (4-Year)
University of Virginia–Charlottesville			●					F	$16,853 / $47,273	88%
University of Virginia–Wise	●	●				●	●	B	$9,825 / $27,055	23%
Virginia Commonwealth University	●					●	●	C	$13,624 / $33,656	39%
Virginia Military Institute	●					●	●	C	$18,214 / $43,902	63%
Virginia Polytechnic Institute	●						●	D	$13,230 / $31,014	63%
Virginia State University	●	●				●	●	B	$8,726 / $19,572	20%
Virginia Union University	●	●				●	●	B	$17,448	16%
Virginia Wesleyan University	●	●	●			●	●	B	$36,660	46%
Washington & Lee University	●		●			●	●	B	$50,170	89%

GENERAL EDUCATION REQUIREMENTS

INSTITUTION	Comp	Lit	Lang	Gov/Hist	Econ	Math	Sci	GRADE	Tuition & Fees* (In-State/Out-of-State)	Graduation** Rate (4-Year)
Central Washington University	●						●	D	$7,903 / $22,010	28%
Eastern Washington University	●					●	●	C	$7,109 / $23,862	25%
Evergreen State College								F	$7,591 / $25,051	42%
Gonzaga University	●						●	D	$41,330	78%
Pacific Lutheran University							●	F	$40,722	58%
Saint Martin's University	●	●		●		●	●	B	$35,656	47%
Seattle Pacific University	●					●	●	C	$40,893	54%
Seattle University	●					●	●	C	$42,885	64%
University of Puget Sound						●	●	D	$48,090	72%
University of Washington–Bothell	●							F	$10,911 / $35,475	43%
University of Washington–Seattle	●					◐	◐	D	$10,974 / $35,538	65%
University of Washington–Tacoma								F	$11,046 / $35,610	40%
Washington State University	●						●	D	$11,391 / $25,817	38%
Western Washington University	●					●	●	C	$8,183 / $22,695	38%

* 2017–18 tuition and fees. Source: U.S. Department of Education's Integrated Postsecondary Education Data System (IPEDS).
** Four-year graduation rates for first-time, full-time freshmen who enrolled in Fall 2011. Source: College Navigator.

GENERAL EDUCATION REQUIREMENTS

INSTITUTION	Comp	Lit	Lang	Gov/ Hist	Econ	Math	Sci	GRADE	Tuition & Fees (In-State/Out-of-State)	Graduation Rate (4-Year)
Whitman College		●					●	D	$49,780	79%
Whitworth University						●	●	D	$42,186	65%

GENERAL EDUCATION REQUIREMENTS

INSTITUTION	Comp	Lit	Lang	Gov/ Hist	Econ	Math	Sci	GRADE	Tuition & Fees* (In-State/Out-of-State)	Graduation** Rate (4-Year)
Alderson Broaddus University	●	●					●	C	$26,610	34%
Bethany College	●	●					●	C	$28,454	35%
Bluefield State College	●	●					●	C	$6,728 / $13,032	11%
Concord University	●	●					●	C	$7,732 / $16,812	18%
Davis & Elkins College	●	●					●	C	$28,992	30%
Fairmont State University	●			●			●	C	$6,950 / $14,666	18%
Glenville State College	●	●					●	C	$7,342 / $16,560	24%
Marshall University							●	F	$7,798 / $17,856	29%
Shepherd University	●					●	●	C	$7,328 / $17,869	25%
West Liberty University	●					●	●	C	$7,380 / $15,020	27%
West Virginia State University	●						●	D	$7,546 / $16,550	10%
West Virginia University	●							F	$8,376 / $23,616	35%
West Virginia Wesleyan College	●	●					●	C	$30,752	38%
Wheeling Jesuit University	●						●	D	$28,110	58%

* *2017–18 tuition and fees. Source: U.S. Department of Education's Integrated Postsecondary Education Data System (IPEDS).*
** *Four-year graduation rates for first-time, full-time freshmen who enrolled in Fall 2011. Source: College Navigator.*

WISCONSIN

GENERAL EDUCATION REQUIREMENTS

INSTITUTION	Comp	Lit	Lang	Gov/Hist	Econ	Math	Sci	GRADE	Tuition & Fees* (In-State/Out-of-State)	Graduation** Rate (4-Year)
Alverno College						●		F	$28,277	11%
Beloit College	●						●	D	$48,706	75%
Cardinal Stritch University	●					●	●	C	$28,844	15%
Carroll University	●					●	●	C	$31,144	52%
Carthage College		●					●	D	$41,950	53%
Concordia University Wisconsin	●	●				●	●	B	$28,600	39%
Lakeland University	●					◖	◖	D	$27,760	44%
Lawrence University			●				●	D	$46,101	65%
Marian University	●	●				●	●	B	$27,400	31%
Marquette University	●							F	$39,900	59%
Ripon College	●							F	$41,835	62%
St. Norbert College						●	●	D	$36,593	69%
University of Wisconsin–Eau Claire	●							F	$8,816 / $16,736	34%
University of Wisconsin–Green Bay							●	F	$7,878 / $15,728	30%
University of Wisconsin–La Crosse	●	●				●	●	B	$9,096 / $17,765	42%

* 2017–18 tuition and fees. Source: U.S. Department of Education's Integrated Postsecondary Education Data System (IPEDS).

** Four-year graduation rates for first-time, full-time freshmen who enrolled in Fall 2011. Source: College Navigator.

GENERAL EDUCATION REQUIREMENTS

INSTITUTION	Comp	Lit	Lang	Gov/ Hist	Econ	Math	Sci	GRADE	Tuition & Fees (In-State/Out-of-State)	Graduation Rate (4-Year)
University of Wisconsin–Madison		●	●				●	C	$10,533 / $34,783	60%
University of Wisconsin–Milwaukee						●	●	D	$9,565 / $20,844	15%
University of Wisconsin–Oshkosh	●					●	●	C	$7,587 / $15,160	19%
University of Wisconsin–Parkside								F	$7,389 / $15,378	10%
University of Wisconsin–Platteville	●					●	●	C	$7,536 / $15,386	19%
University of Wisconsin–River Falls	●						●	D	$8,013 / $15,586	28%
University of Wisconsin–Stevens Point	●						●	D	$8,209 / $16,476	33%
University of Wisconsin–Superior	●	●				●	●	B	$8,109 / $15,682	24%
University of Wisconsin–Whitewater	●	●					●	C	$7,662 / $16,235	32%
Wisconsin Lutheran College	●	●				●	●	B	$29,140	50%

WYOMING

GENERAL EDUCATION REQUIREMENTS

INSTITUTION	Comp	Lit	Lang	Gov/ Hist	Econ	Math	Sci	GRADE	Tuition & Fees* (In-State/Out-of-State)	Graduation** Rate (4-Year)
University of Wyoming	●			●			●	C	$5,217 / $16,827	26%

* *2017–18 tuition and fees. Source: U.S. Department of Education's Integrated Postsecondary Education Data System (IPEDS).*
** *Four-year graduation rates for first-time, full-time freshmen who enrolled in Fall 2011. Source: College Navigator.*